Unity Character Animation with Mecanim

A detailed guide to the complex new animation tools in Unity, packed with clear instructions and illustrated with original content in the context of a next generation zombie apocalypse adventure game

Jamie Dean

[PACKT] PUBLISHING

BIRMINGHAM - MUMBAI

D1504844

Unity Character Animation with Mecanim

First published: September 2015

Production reference: 1230915

Published by Packt Publishing Ltd.
Livery Place
35 Livery Street
Birmingham B3 2PB, UK.

ISBN 978-1-84969-636-4

www.packtpub.com

Cover image by Suresh Mogre (suresh.mogre.99@gmail.com)

Credits

Author

Jamie Dean

Reviewers

Shaad Boochoon

Ashley Egan

Brian Gatt

Adam Ormsby

Acquisition Editor

Aaron Lazar

Content Development Editor

Athira Laji

Technical Editor

Prajakta Mhatre

Copy Editor

Charlotte Carneiro

Project Coordinator

Harshal Ved

Proofreader

Safis Editing

Indexer

Rekha Nair

Production Coordinator

Aparna Bhagat

Cover Work

Aparna Bhagat

About the Author

Jamie Dean is a game artist, developer, instructor, and freelancer, with over 7 years of teaching experience in higher education and developing 3D content for game projects.

About the Reviewers

Shaad Boochoon was born and raised in Trinidad and Tobago. He studied systems engineering at the Southern Alberta Institute of Technology in Calgary, Canada. After working in software development, he decided to enter the video game industry and did visual and creative arts. He is a post-graduate in game level design at Sheridan College in Toronto, Canada. Shaad is currently a lead game designer at Vertical Depth Studios in Toronto.

Ashley Egan is an animation artist living in Chicago, Illinois with her cat, Charlie. She attended Columbia College Chicago and received her bachelors of arts in game design with a specialization in game art. From motion capture to game engines, Ashley strives to learn about different animation software and tools.

> I'd like to thank Adam Ormsby, who went on a journey with me into the world of Mecanim, and now I don't want to leave.

Brian Gatt is a software developer who holds a bachelor's degree in computer science and artificial intelligence from the University of Malta and a master's degree in computer games and entertainment from Goldsmiths, University of London. Having initially dabbled with OpenGL at university, he has since developed an interest in graphics programming. In his spare time, he likes to keep up with the latest graphic APIs, native C++ programming, and game development techniques.

Adam Ormsby is a technical game designer currently developing games for PC and mobile platforms using the Unity engine. His main work is designing and implementing gameplay systems, and he has developed a special love for scripting character and environment animation behaviors using Mecanim.

Adam is a member of The MecWarriors, a group of talented developers whose goal is to build time-saving plugins and packages for Mecanim. They write Mecanim tutorials on their blog at `www.mecwarriors.com`, and they'd love for you to visit.

I'd like to thank Jason Parks for inspiring me to start The MecWarriors group and Ashley Egan for jumping down that rabbit hole with me.

www.PacktPub.com

Support files, eBooks, discount offers, and more

For support files and downloads related to your book, please visit www.PacktPub.com.

Did you know that Packt offers eBook versions of every book published, with PDF and ePub files available? You can upgrade to the eBook version at www.PacktPub.com and as a print book customer, you are entitled to a discount on the eBook copy. Get in touch with us at service@packtpub.com for more details.

At www.PacktPub.com, you can also read a collection of free technical articles, sign up for a range of free newsletters and receive exclusive discounts and offers on Packt books and eBooks.

https://www2.packtpub.com/books/subscription/packtlib

Do you need instant solutions to your IT questions? PacktLib is Packt's online digital book library. Here, you can search, access, and read Packt's entire library of books.

Why subscribe?

- Fully searchable across every book published by Packt
- Copy and paste, print, and bookmark content
- On demand and accessible via a web browser

Free access for Packt account holders

If you have an account with Packt at www.PacktPub.com, you can use this to access PacktLib today and view 9 entirely free books. Simply use your login credentials for immediate access.

Table of Contents

Preface	**vii**
Chapter 1: The Zombie Attacks!	**1**
Setting up the project	**1**
Importing our enemy	2
Organizing the material and textures	3
Adjusting the import scale	4
Adjusting the rig import settings and creating the Avatar	7
Setting up the animator controller	13
Creating states	15
Creating a parameter	16
Adding transitions	17
Writing the script	19
Adjusting the scene elements to preview the animation	21
Previewing the hit animation in the game view	21
Summary	**22**
Chapter 2: Rigging Characters for Unity in 3ds Max and Maya	**23**
Understanding the need for rigging	**23**
Minimum requirements	**24**
Sourcing models	**25**
Modeling for animation	**25**
Rigging in 3ds Max	**26**
Setting up the scene	26
Importing the character model	27
Creating the Biped system	28
Adjusting the Biped's parameters	29
Adjusting the Biped to fit the character	30
Switching to X-ray mode and freezing the character mesh	31
Adjusting limb positions	35
Renaming bones	36
Copying and pasting the position, rotation, and scale data from one side to the other	36

Skinning the character using the skin modifier 38
  Creating a selection set 40
  Saving the default pose 40
  Creating the test pose 41
  Making adjustments to the Skin modifier 44
Exporting the rigged character 53
Rigging in Maya **54**
Setting up Maya to rig our character model 54
  Setting system units to meters 55
  Changing the display grid size 55
  Importing the model 55
  Adjusting the model scale 56
  Adjusting the viewport display and toolset for joint creation 57
  Creating joints for the back, neck, and head 58
  Renaming and repositioning the joints 59
Creating the leg joints 60
Creating the arm joints 61
  Cloning the finger joints 63
Mirroring joints for the leg and arm chains 64
  Connecting the arm and leg chains 65
  Creating the ponytail and jaw joints 65
  Aligning joint transforms 66
  Creating a test pose 67
Binding the character mesh to the skeleton 69
Painting skin weights 71
Exporting for unity 73
Summary **74**
Chapter 3: Interacting with the Environment **75**
Importing the project assets package **76**
Setting up the player character 76
Creating a new scene 77
Adding the player character model to the scene 77
Adding the character controller 78
  Adjusting the camera height 80
Adding the shoot idle animation 81
  Adding and parenting the gun 82
  Saving the first-person rig as a prefab 84
  Adding the office-level scene 84
  Completing the camera setup 86
  Modifying the animator controller 87
  Setting the transition 87
Writing and implementing the character animation script 89
Adding the initial code to the FPSAnimation script 89
Adding the script to the player character game object 91

Adding and implementing collectable objects   **92**

Instantiating the lunchBox collectable in the game level   92

Inspecting the lunchBox collectable's components   93

Setting up the player character's response   95

Adding the Pickup state to the animator controller   96

Creating the pickup camera   98

Finalizing the pickup camera prefab   98

Looking at the player status script   100

Updating the Collectable script   101

Updating the FPSAnimation script   104

Modifying the pickup script   104

Testing the lunchBox collectable   108

Summary   **109**

Chapter 4: Working with Motion Capture Data   **111**

Introduction to motion capture sequences and their characteristics   **112**

Using a motion capture sequence with a pre-rigged model   **113**

Getting started   113

Importing the motion capture sequence   114

Adjusting the import settings   114

Adjusting the sequence in the Animations tab   118

Creating the second walk cycle   121

Adding the new motion clips to the animation controller   122

Creating a script to see both animation loops in action   123

Summary   **125**

Chapter 5: Retargeting Animation   **127**

Loading the scene   **128**

Adding and previewing the animation   128

Adjusting import settings to get a better fit   130

Creating a duplicate walk cycle   131

Adjusting the motion parameters   131

Adjusting the muscle limits   134

Working with Avatar Body Masks   138

Opening the new scene   138

Creating a second layer in the animator controller   142

Creating states in the mask layer   143

Setting the parameter and transitions in the mask layer   144

Editing the script   144

Previewing the masked animation   145

Creating five walk variations from two walk cycles   **146**

Adding more Avatar masks   **147**

Summary   **149**

Chapter 6: Talking Heads — **151**

Adding the snarl face animation to the female zombie character — **152**
Setting the scene in Unity — 152
Adding code to the zombie_ready script — **152**
Adding the TurnToPlayer function — 154
Connecting the variables in the Inspector panel — 155
Updating the animator controller to include the face animation — **156**
Adding the Snarl state — 157
Creating a Null state — 158
Setting transitions between the Null and Snarl states — 159
Creating the IsSnarling parameter — 160
Editing the script to include the Face layer — 160
Smoothing the zombie's turn rotation — 162
Implementing the turn animation — **163**
Adding the turning state — 163
Setting up the IsTurning parameter — 164
Creating the transitions to connect the turning state — 165
Setting the transitions for the Turn state — 165
Updating the zombie_ready script to accommodate the Turn state — 166
Driving a blendshape animation with the animator controller — **172**
Viewing the blendshape in Unity — 173
Keyframing the face blendshape — 175
Updating the animator to handle the blendshape animation — 177
Summary — **180**

Chapter 7: Controlling Player Animation with Blend Trees — **181**

Adding a Blend Tree to the player's existing animator controller — **182**
Adding strafing animation to the player character with a Blend Tree — 182
Using Blend Tree properties — 183
Adding the motion clips to the Blend Tree — 184
Adding and adjusting the Blend Tree parameters and thresholds — 185
Updating the character script to use the Blend Tree — 187
Testing the Blend Tree in the Game View — 188
Varying the pickup animation with a Blend Tree — **189**
Viewing the pickup_heavy animation sequence — 190
Creating a Blend Tree in the Pickup state — 191
Setting the pickup Blend Tree parameter — 192
Setting the threshold for the pickup Blend Tree — 192
Editing the character animation script to accommodate
the pickup Blend Tree — 193
Updating the Collectable script to include a weight variable — 194
Sending the objectWeight variable — 195
Updating the Pick function in the character animation script — 195

Testing the blended animation in the game 196
Instancing the collectable prefabs 196
Previewing the blended animation 198
Summary **199**
Chapter 8: Implementing Ragdoll Physics **201**
Introduction to joints in Unity **202**
Creating a test scene 202
Adding a hinge joint 204
Creating the ragdoll object **206**
Assigning the material 208
Generating the initial ragdoll 209
Adjusting collision objects 212
Fine-tuning the character joints 217
Adjusting the rotational limits of the head 220
Adding a custom joint to the ragdoll 221
Saving the ragdoll as a prefab 224
Summary **224**
Chapter 9: Controlling Enemy Animation with AI and Triggers **225**
Implementing range detection **225**
Looking at the scene 226
Adding the initial AI script 227
Adding proximity detection to the enemy AI script 227
Setting up the patrol behavior 229
Adding variables for the patrol 230
Adding the initial patrol code to the update function 231
Defining patrol points 234
Modifying the animator 236
Adding and accessing an animation curve 237
Accessing the animation curve in Mecanim and using it in the script 239
Adding the attack 241
Adding the Attack state 242
Associating tags with the enemy and player game objects 244
Allowing the zombie to hurt the player 245
Damaging and killing the zombie 246
Allowing the player to fire 248
Pathfinding and obstacle detection with navMesh **250**
Suspending navigation during the turn 253
Adjusting navigation during the attack 254
Modifying the Attack function 254
Timing out the zombie's pursuit **256**
Summary **258**
Index **261**

Preface

In the past few years, Unity has proved itself to be a versatile, user-friendly platform for game production and other interactive applications. With it, developers can rapidly assemble game menus and interfaces, build levels, animate characters, and define how these elements interact with each other.

Compared to other development tools, Unity is artist-friendly, centering on a Scene viewport window and controls that will be familiar to anyone who has worked with 3D software. Like all game engines, it requires scripting to enable any complex functionality, but coding can quickly be tested and adjusted making for a less-frustrating experience for anyone from a non-programming background.

Unity's easy-to-learn drag and drop functionality has endeared it to enthusiasts and professionals alike. Its multiplatform publishing capabilities streamlined the creation of all sorts of games played on PC, Mac, iOS, Android and consoles.

The personal edition of Unity can be downloaded for free, making it suitable for entry-level game developers. The online manual and scripting reference, in addition to the thriving developer community, make it easy to find support and get queries answered.

The addition of Mecanim to Unity gives the independent game developer an even more expansive toolset, making it possible to handle a significant part of the character animation process without the use of additional software. It makes retargeting, retiming, and adjusting existing animations a simple task without the usual problems that accompany importing and exporting data between applications.

The modeling toolset within Unity is extremely limited — primitive objects such as spheres, cubes, and planes can be assembled — but if it is the actual modeling and texturing of characters and levels that you are most interested in, you will need a general 3D package such as 3ds Max, Maya, or blender. These aspects of building a game are well addressed in other publications.

The context

In order to closely correspond to the development of a real game, the projects in this book follow a theme of a typical first-person action game—the sort that is often found to be played on PC, console, and mobile platforms—the context is the zombie apocalypse. During the game, our player must negotiate his or her way out of an office complex full of zombies. In terms of character animation, this will offer us plenty of variety in the type of movement required by the player and enemies.

What this book covers

This book will take the reader through the different processes involved in the character animation aspect of game development. It will explain the basic animation tools within Unity, as well as the dynamic Mecanim toolset and how it can be used in the game animation context.

Chapter 1, The Zombie Attacks!, introduces the Mecanim interface and explains how rigged characters can be imported to Unity and quickly set up with animation.

Chapter 2, Rigging Characters for Unity in 3ds Max and Maya, explains the relationship between the Unity engine and commonly used 3D software and how characters can be prepared within external software to function smoothly once imported to Unity.

Chapter 3, Interacting with the Environment, compares a few different strategies for making a character interact convincingly with the environment.

Chapter 4, Working with Motion Capture Data, walks you through the process of adapting motion capture files to animate your character with Mecanim's toolset.

Chapter 5, Retargeting Animation, considers the reuse of animation clips and how animation can be adapted within Unity to suit different character types.

Chapter 6, Talking Heads, demonstrates Mecanim's facial animation capabilities and the scripting necessary to get these working in a game.

Chapter 7, Controlling Player Animation with Blend Trees, explores more of the advanced features of the Animator panel, defining smooth blending between different animation clips with a limited implementation of scripting.

Chapter 8, Implementing Ragdoll Physics, compares the use of real-world physics with the character controller component and how these can both be implemented in a character setup.

Chapter 9, Controlling Enemy Animation with AI and Triggers, demonstrates how scripted behavior and Unity's navMesh navigation system can be used to control enemy character animations within a game.

What the book does not cover

Modeling, texturing of assets in 3D software, scripting game states, and GUI within Unity. These aspects of game development are beyond the scope of this book.

What you need for this book

Understanding key animation concepts is necessary to complete the chapters in this book. In addition, you will need the following:

- Unity 5 installed on your machine (Mac or PC). The free personal version of the software is sufficient for all of the project content in this book. This can be downloaded from the Unity webpage.

- A little understanding of 3D software, x, y, and z coordinates, translating, rotating, and scaling elements within the Unity viewer interface.

- A basic understanding of Unityscript or C# will be helpful to complete the projects, though the code that is included is clearly explained.

- Additional 3D software is useful, but not required. The industry standards Autodesk Maya and 3ds Max both have free 30-day trials, which can be downloaded from the main Autodesk website. Blender is a free alternative.

Who this book is for

This book focuses on the character animation aspect of game production in Unity.

If you are completely new to Unity, it is recommended to read through some of the basic introductory material documentation on the official site. If you have experience working with an older version of the software, then this book should give you a good idea of how Mecanim can be used in your pipeline.

If you are new to animation, this book uses some character animation terminology that you may not be familiar with. Where possible, I have explained these terms.

My approach to writing this book comes from an artist, rather than coder background. If your motivation for understanding character animation in Unity is to showcase your artwork in a demo or even a full-scale game, you have come to the right place!

Conventions

In this book, you will find a number of text styles that distinguish between different kinds of information. Here are some examples of these styles and an explanation of their meaning.

Code words in text, database table names, folder names, filenames, file extensions, pathnames, dummy URLs, user input, and Twitter handles are shown as follows: "Choose an appropriate file name for the scene, such as `Chapter1_1`."

A block of code is set as follows:

```
var health : int = 10;
var healthLimit : int = 10;

function AddHealth (increase : int)
{
    health += increase;

    if (health > healthLimit)
{
        health = healthLimit;
    }
```

New terms and important words are shown in bold. Words that you see on the screen, for example, in menus or dialog boxes, appear in the text like this: "Click on the **Model** tab."

> Warnings or important notes appear in a box like this.

> Tips and tricks appear like this.

Reader feedback

Feedback from our readers is always welcome. Let us know what you think about this book—what you liked or disliked. Reader feedback is important for us as it helps us develop titles that you will really get the most out of.

To send us general feedback, simply e-mail feedback@packtpub.com, and mention the book's title in the subject of your message.

If there is a topic that you have expertise in and you are interested in either writing or contributing to a book, see our author guide at www.packtpub.com/authors.

Customer support

Now that you are the proud owner of a Packt book, we have a number of things to help you to get the most from your purchase.

Downloading the example code

You can download the example code files from your account at http://www.packtpub.com for all the Packt Publishing books you have purchased. If you purchased this book elsewhere, you can visit http://www.packtpub.com/support and register to have the files e-mailed directly to you.

Downloading the color images of this book

We also provide you with a PDF file that has color images of the screenshots/diagrams used in this book. The color images will help you better understand the changes in the output. You can download this file from:

https://www.packtpub.com/sites/default/files/downloads/B03192_ColoredImages.pdf

Errata

Although we have taken every care to ensure the accuracy of our content, mistakes do happen. If you find a mistake in one of our books — maybe a mistake in the text or the code — we would be grateful if you could report this to us. By doing so, you can save other readers from frustration and help us improve subsequent versions of this book. If you find any errata, please report them by visiting http://www.packtpub.com/submit-errata, selecting your book, clicking on the **Errata Submission Form** link, and entering the details of your errata. Once your errata are verified, your submission will be accepted and the errata will be uploaded to our website or added to any list of existing errata under the Errata section of that title.

To view the previously submitted errata, go to https://www.packtpub.com/books/content/support and enter the name of the book in the search field. The required information will appear under the **Errata** section.

Piracy

Piracy of copyrighted material on the Internet is an ongoing problem across all media. At Packt, we take the protection of our copyright and licenses very seriously. If you come across any illegal copies of our works in any form on the Internet, please provide us with the location address or website name immediately so that we can pursue a remedy.

Please contact us at copyright@packtpub.com with a link to the suspected pirated material.

We appreciate your help in protecting our authors and our ability to bring you valuable content.

Questions

If you have a problem with any aspect of this book, you can contact us at questions@packtpub.com, and we will do our best to address the problem.

1
The Zombie Attacks!

In this chapter, we will demonstrate the process of importing and animating a rigged character in Unity. After making sure the character is being imported correctly, we will work through the necessary steps to get the character animated in the game view using the Mecanim toolset and a little code.

In this chapter we will cover:

- Starting a blank Unity project and importing the necessary packages
- Importing a rigged character model in the FBX format and adjusting import settings
- Organizing materials and textures within the project hierarchy
- Setting up the Avatar using the Avatar Definition Mapping panel
- Creating a simple state machine in the animator controller panel
- The basics of scripting for Mecanim

Typically, an enemy character such as this will have a series of different animation sequences, which will be imported separately or together from a 3D package. In this case, our animation sequences are included in separate files.

We will begin, by creating the Unity project.

Setting up the project

Before we start exploring the animation workflow with Mecanim's tools, we need to set up the Unity project:

1. Create a new project within Unity by navigating to **File | New Project...**.
2. When prompted, choose an appropriate name and location for the project.

3. In the **Unity - Project Wizard** dialog that appears, check the relevant boxes for the **Character Controller.unityPackage** and **Scripts.unityPackage** packages.

4. Click on the **Create** button. It may take a few minutes for Unity to initialize.

5. Download the project ZIP file for this book from the Packt website. The file contains a Unity assets package with the content necessary for the projects in this book.

Downloading the example code

You can download the example code files from your account at http://www.packtpub.com for all the Packt Publishing books you have purchased. If you purchased this book elsewhere, you can visit http://www.packtpub.com/support and register to have the files e-mailed directly to you.

6. When the Unity interface appears, import the PACKT_CAWM package by navigating to **Assets | Import Package | Custom Package...**.

7. The **Import package...** window will appear.

8. Navigate to the location where you unzipped the project files, select the unity package, and click on **Open**.

The assets package will take a little time to decompress.

9. When the **Importing Package** checklist appears, click on the **Import** button in the bottom-right of the window.

Once the assets have finished importing, you will start with a default blank scene.

Importing our enemy

Now, it is time to import our character model:

1. Minimize Unity.

2. Navigate to the location where you unzipped the project files.

3. Double-click on the **Models** folder to view its contents.

4. Double-click on the zombie_m subfolder to view its contents.

The folder contains an FBX file containing the rigged male zombie model and a separate subfolder containing the associated textures.

5. Open Unity and resize the window so that both Unity and the zombie_m folder contents are visible.

6. In Unity, click on the **Assets** folder in the **Project** panel.

7. Drag the `zombie_m` FBX asset into the **Assets** panel to import it.

   Because the FBX file contains a normal map, a window will pop up asking if you want to set this file's import settings to read it correctly.

8. Click on the **Fix Now** button.

 FBX files can contain embedded bitmap textures, which can be imported with the model. This will create subfolders containing the materials and textures within the folder where the model has been imported. Leaving the materials and textures as subfolders of the model will make them difficult to find within the project.

The zombie model and two folders should now be visible in the `FBX_Imports` folder in the **Assets** panel.

In the next step, we will move the imported material and texture assets into the appropriate folders in the Unity project.

Organizing the material and textures

The material and textures associated with the `zombie_m` model are currently located within the `FBX_Imports` folder. We will move these into different folders to organize them within the hierarchy of our project:

1. Double-click on the `Materials` folder and drag the material asset contained within it into the `PACKT_Materials` folder in the **Project** panel.

2. Return to the `FBX_Imports` folder by clicking on its title at the top of the **Assets** panel interface.

3. Double-click on the textures folder. This will be named to be consistent with the model.

4. Drag the two bitmap textures into the `PACKT_Textures` folder in the **Project** panel.

5. Return to the `FBX_Imports` folder and delete the two empty subfolders.

   The moved material and textures will still be linked to the model. We will make sure of this by instancing it in the current empty scene.

6. Drag the `zombie_m` asset into the **Hierarchy** panel.

It may not be immediately visible within the **Scene** view due to the default import scale settings.

We will take care of this in the next step.

Adjusting the import scale

Unity's import settings can be adjusted to account for the different tools commonly used to create 2D and 3D assets. Import settings are adjusted in the **Inspector** panel, which will appear on the right of the unity interface by default:

1. Click on the `zombie_m` game object within the **Hierarchy** panel.

    This will bring up the file's import settings in the **Inspector** panel.

2. Click on the **Model** tab.

3. In the **Scale Factor** field, highlight the current number and type 1.

 The character model has been modeled to scale in *meters* to make it compatible with Unity's units. All 3D software applications have their own native scale. Unity does a pretty good job at accommodating all of them, but it often helps to know which software was used to create them.

4. Scroll down until the **Materials** settings are visible.

5. Uncheck the **Import Materials** checkbox.

    Now that we have got our textures and materials organized within the project, we want to make sure they are not continuously imported into the same folder as the model.

6. Leave the remaining **Model Import** settings at their default values.

   We will be discussing these later on in the book, when we demonstrate the animation import.

7. Click on the **Apply** button. You may need to scroll down within the **Inspector** panel to see this:

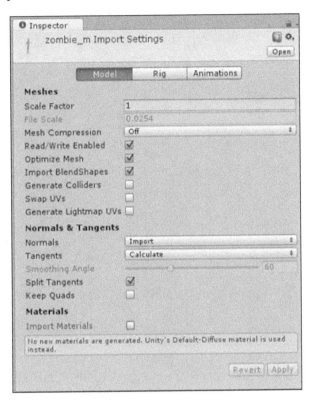

The zombie_m character should now be visible in the **Scene** view:

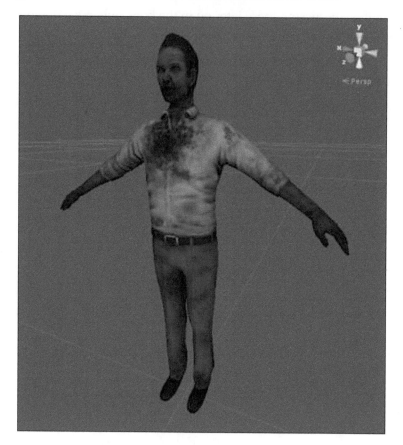

This character model is a medium resolution model — 4410 triangles and has a single 1024 x 1024 albedo texture and separate 1024 x 1024 specular and normal maps.

The character has been rigged with a basic skeleton. Creating a skeletal rig will be discussed in detail in the next chapter. The rigging process is essential if the model is to be animated.

We need to save our progress, before we get any further:

1. Save the scene by navigating to **File | Save Scene as...**.
2. Choose an appropriate filename for the scene, such as Chapter1_1.
3. Click on the **Apply** button.

Despite the fact that we have only added a single game object to the default scene, there are more steps that we will need to take to set up the character and it will be convenient for us to save the current set up in case anything goes wrong.

In the character animation, there are looping and single-shot animation sequences. Some animation sequences such as walk, run, idle are usually seamless loops designed to play back-to-back without the player being aware of where they start and end.

Other sequences, typically, shooting, hitting, being injured or dying are often single-shot animations, which do not need to loop. We will start with this kind, and discuss looping animation sequences later in the book.

In order to use Mecanim's animation tools, we need to set up the character's Avatar so that the character's hierarchy of bones is recognized and can be used correctly within Unity.

Adjusting the rig import settings and creating the Avatar

Now that we have imported the model, we will need to adjust the import settings so that the character functions correctly within our scene:

1. Select zombie_m in the **Assets** panel
2. The asset's import settings should become visible within the **Inspector** panel.
3. This settings rollout contains three tabs: **Model**, **Rig**, and **Animations**.
4. Since we have already adjusted the **Scale Factor** within the **Model Import** settings, we will move on to the **Rig** import settings where we can define what kind of skeleton our character has.

Choosing the appropriate rig import settings

Mecanim has three options for importing rigged models: **Legacy**, **Generic**, and **Humanoid**. It also has a *none* option that should be applied to models that are not intended to be animated.

Legacy format was previously the only option for importing skeletal animation in Unity. It is not possible to retarget animation sequences between models using Legacy, and setting up functioning state machines requires quite a bit of scripting. It is still a useful tool for importing models with fewer animation sequences and for simple mechanical animations. Legacy format animations are not compatible with Mecanim.

Generic is one of the new animation formats that are compatible with Mecanim's animator controllers. It does not have the full functionality of Mecanim's character animation tools. Animations sequences imported with the generic format cannot be retargeted and are best used for quadrupeds, mechanical devices, pretty much anything except a character with two arms and two legs.

The **Humanoid** animation type allows the full use of Mecanim's powerful toolset. It requires a minimum of 15 bones, and assumes that your rig is roughly human shaped with a pair of arms and legs. It can accommodate many more intermediary joints and some basic facial animation.

One of the greatest benefits of using the **Humanoid** type is that it allows animation sequences to be retargeted or adapted to work with different rigs. For instance, you may have a detailed player character model with a full skeletal rig (including fingers and toes joints), maybe you want to reuse this character's idle sequence with a background character that is much less detailed, and has a simpler arrangement of bones.

Mecanim makes it possible reuse purpose built motion sequences and even create useable sequences from motion capture data.

Now that we have introduced these three rig types, we need to choose the appropriate setting for our imported zombie character, which in this case is **Humanoid**:

1. In the **Inspector** panel, click on the **Rig** tab.
2. Set the **Animation Type** field to Humanoid to suit our character skeleton type.
3. Leave **Avatar Definition** set to **Create From This Model**.
4. **Optimize Game Objects** can be left checked.
5. Click on the **Apply** button to save the settings and transfer all of the changes that you have made to the instance in the scene.

This is how the screenshot will look like:

The **Humanoid** animation type is the only one that supports retargeting. So if you are importing animations that are not unique and will be used for multiple characters, it is a good idea to use this setting.

In the next step, we will define the hierarchy of the joints in the Avatar.

Creating the Avatar

The **Avatar Mapping** settings allow you to specify how the bones relate to the model. You can think of the Avatar as an intermediary device that translates between the character model and the animations. It will dictate how motion will be transferred to the model, so it is important that all of the models bones are correctly identified within the hierarchy.

1. In the **Inspector** panel, click on the **Configure...** button to bring up the **Avatar Mapping** settings.

   Unity will prompt you to save your scene, which is necessary because the Avatar definition is actually done in a separate, temporary scene.

2. Click on the **Save Scene** button.

   The **Avatar Definition** panel will become active in the **Inspector** panel.

   The **Mapping** tab should be active by default. This shows a simplified diagram of a humanoid bone hierarchy. Beneath the diagram is a list where bones are selected.

3. Choose the **Mapping** rollout in the bottom left of the panel.

4. Click on **Automap**, Unity will attempt to assign the bones to the slots in the **Avatar** based on their names and position within the hierarchy.

Because our character's skeleton uses recognized naming conventions, Unity should have automatically put each bone into the right slot within the mapping definition. Any unidentified positions will show up in *red*, and any non-essential or optional bones that have not been identified will be displayed in *gray*.

Above the actual bone definition slots, there are alternate tabs for the body, head, left hand, and right hand, where more joints can be defined for more detailed rigs. With the exception of the head and neck, the bones covered under the **Head** tab are not that important right now. Facial animation will be covered later, in *Chapter 6, Talking Heads*.

The rest of the bones in the list for body, left hand, and right hand will need to be allocated. You can scroll down in the panel to see the names of the bones from your hierarchy and which position they have been placed in within the Avatar.

Note that the Avatar mapping definition only has two positions available for spine bones, if the character you are mapping has more than two bones in its spine (like this example), you can decide which of them to use.

I usually leave out the upper-spine bone, as it typically contains very little data in animation sequences, and because of its proximity to the neck and shoulders, which usually have more influence on the vertices of the model.

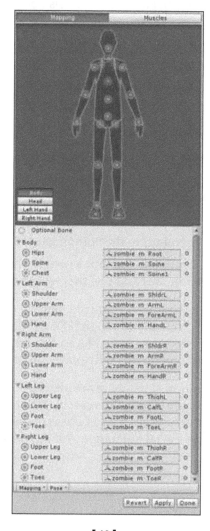

A common occurrence at this point of the process is a red warning display in your **Scene** view notifying you that the character is not in T-pose:

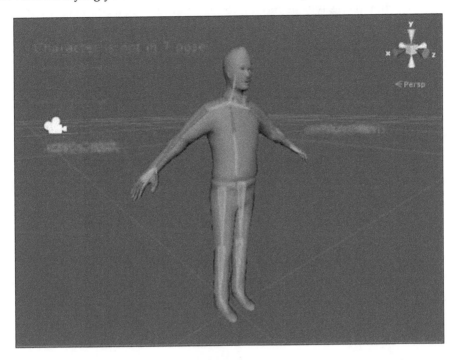

This is a simple fix, as we will demonstrate in the next step.

Adjusting the character's pose

Mecanim requires character models to be in a T-pose for them to be properly processed. The true T-pose is not a universal default pose for character models, and luckily Mecanim has a way to accommodate this:

1. Click on the **Pose** rollout at the bottom of the **Avatar Mapping** tab within the **Inspector** panel.

2. Choose **Enforce T-pose**. This will force your characters arms into a true T-pose so that they are Mecanim compatible.

You may wonder why we don't just model a character in a T-pose rather than something more like an M. The main reason is that, while it is on the screen, the character's arms will usually be down by its side, modeling the arms at 45 degrees rather than 90 will minimize the amount of stretching of the mesh and textures.

Dedicated motion editing packages, such as Autodesk MotionBuilder, also require a true T-pose, so the **Enforce T-Pose** option within Mecanim is a good compromise and a nice touch, which saves us having to remodel or rerig a character in order to use these tools.

Checking the bone hierarchy in the Avatar

Mecanim's Avatar definition tools are responsive to bone hierarchy and naming conventions. If you are working with several character rigs that have the same bone names, it is likely you will only need to tweak the settings the first time.

The tool sometimes goes wrong. When this is the case, make sure you follow these steps:

1. Once you initiate the mapping process, the skeleton in your **Hierarchy** panel is expanded to make it easy to drag and drop. All you have to do is drag the bones from the **Hierarchy** panel into the appropriate slot in the list.

2. Take the time to check the bones in the list to make sure that there are no mistakes.

3. Optional bones, such as the neck and toes, are quite often left out by the automatic mapping, so it is a good idea to add them (in the appropriate definition slots), at this stage, before you apply the settings.

 If you make a mistake, just drag the correct bone onto the field in the list to replace it.

4. When you are finished, click on **Done**. This will save the settings of the Avatar and apply them to the instance of the model in the scene.

The Avatar asset will now be referenced in the **Animator** component of the character game object, which can be viewed in the **Inspector** panel:

At this point, our Avatar is configured, creating a link to our character's skeleton hierarchy that Unity can use.

Next, we will lay the ground work to add a simple animation that will run in the game.

Setting up the animator controller

Mecanim requires an animator controller to connect compatible animation clips with the character model. This is displayed as a node-based interface, which shows the relationships between different animation clips and the parameters that trigger them.

We can continue with the scene, or if you have closed Unity since working on the last section, re-open the scene that you saved. You can open the scene by navigating to **File | Open Scene | PACKT_Scenes | Chapter1_1**.

Assets imported with animation will have space for an animator controller to be added to them. Follow these steps to create the controller:

1. Click on the PACKT_Controllers folder in the **Project** panel.
2. Navigate to **Create | Animator Controller**.
3. The **Animator Controller** icon will appear in the **Assets** panel in the lower-center of the interface.
4. Rename this zombieControl.
5. Click on the **Animator** tab to open the **Animator** panel. If this is not visible, add it in the menu bar by navigating to **Window | Animator**.
6. Drag the **Animator** tab above its current position to undock it as a window.

 Undocking the **Animator** panel is not strictly necessary, especially if you are working with on a large monitor, but it will give you more space to view the whole state machine as it is created.

In the newly created animator controller, there are two visible states, labeled **Entry** and **Any State**:

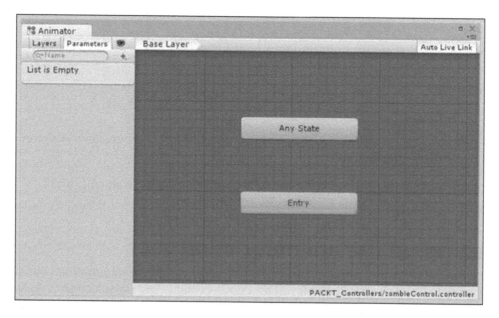

The **Entry** state will usually be the starting point when the game starts or when the character is instantiated. We can use **Any State** to override states, which are currently running if we want something else to take priority.

Setting up a number of states for animation clips will enable greater control over the implementation of the animated sequences. We will add more states in the next step.

Creating states

States are the building blocks of the animator controller. Each state includes one or more motion clip. States are linked using **Transitions**, visually presenting the order in which states will become active:

1. Create a new state by right-clicking on the empty part of the animator graph.

2. Navigate to **Create State | Empty**.

3. Select the state by clicking on it. Rename it Idle in the **Inspector** panel.

4. Create a second state in the same way. Name this Hit in the **Inspector** panel.

Next, we will add the appropriate animation clips to the states:

1. Click on the PACKT_Animations folder within the **Project** panel.

2. In the **Assets** panel, expand both the zombie_idle and zombie_attack animation assets by clicking on the small arrow on the right side of their icons.

3. Select the **Idle** state in the **Animator** window.

4. Drag the zombie_idle animation to the **Motion** slot in the **Inspector** panel:

5. Select the **Hit** state and drag the `hit` animation from the expanded `zombie_attack` asset into the **Motion** slot in the **Inspector** panel:

These animations are now tied to the states that we have set up.

At the moment, the states are unconnected. To connect them, you need to create a parameter that will define the conditions that cause the character to switch to another state.

Creating a parameter

In the **Animator** interface, parameters are used to specify when states will run. They are similar to variables in Unity scripts and can take the form of integers, floats, and booleans. To create a parameter follow these steps:

1. In the upper-left of the **Animator** window, click on the **Parameters** tab and the + symbol to create a new parameter.

2. Choose **Trigger** from the list.

    In Mecanim, a trigger parameter allows you to allow a quick action. It is ideal for attack states because it is reset each time it is fired off.

3. Name the parameter `Hits`

This trigger parameter will determine when the zombie's attack animation will play.

Adding transitions

The next stage is to create transitions between your two states. Transitions show how states are connected in the **Animator** window:

1. Right click on the **Idle** state in the **Animator** window.

2. Select **Make Transition**.

3. Click once on the **Hit** state.

The transition is displayed as a white line with an arrow indicating its direction:

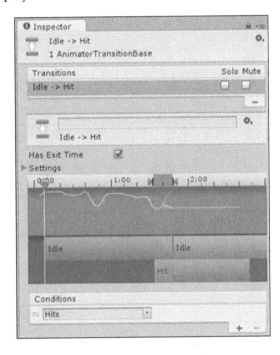

We also need to create a transition from **Hit** back to **Idle**, so the character will stop playing this animation:

1. Right click on **Hit** and click once on **Idle** to create the return transition.

    In the animator controller, it is the transitions that contain the parameters.

2. Click once on the transition pointing from **Idle** to **Hit**. Its setting will appear in the **Inspector** panel.

    The only change that needs to be made to the default settings, at this stage, is to change the drop down in the **Conditions** box at the bottom of the panel.

3. Click on the arrow and select the Hits parameter from the list.

As we want the full attack animation to play out, we will leave the **Conditions** box in the return transition with its default setting **Exit Time**. This will set the state to transition out once the animation has played through:

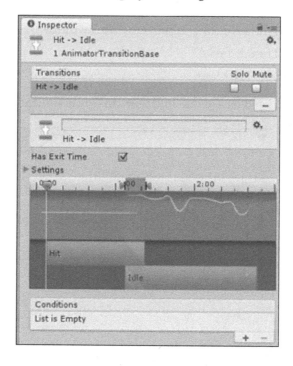

The **Animation** controller is now complete. We will add it to the male zombie character in the next step:

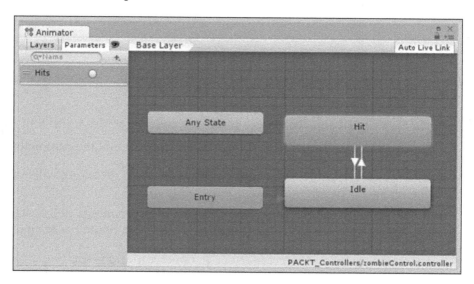

1. Select the `zombie_m` game object in the **Hierarchy** panel.

2. Drag the `zombie_control` animator controller onto the **Controller** slot in the character's **Animator** component.

At this stage, when we test the game, the zombie will run its idle animation, as its **Idle** state is currently specified as the default state (marked in orange in the **Animator** window).

In order to enable the **Hit** state to take over, we will need to do a little scripting.

Writing the script

The character requires a small amount of code to enable it to switch to its **Hit** state and play the `zombie_hit` animation:

1. Select the `PACKT_Scripts` folder in the **Project** panel.

2. Create a new Javascript file by navigating to **Create | Javascript**.

3. Rename the file `zombie_attack`.

4. Double-click on the file to open it in MonoDevelop.

5. At the top of the script, add the following code:

```
var thisAnimator : Animator;
```

This is a variable, which is used to keep track of the character's animator controller that is attached as a component to the same game object that we will attach this script to.

> If you are coding in C#, rather than Javascript, the syntax is a little different. Functions are defined with the prefix `void` rather than function and variables are defined without the `var` prefix and with their type before their name, without the separating colon, such as this:
> `Animator thisAnimator;`
>
> You will find the completed code (in both languages), in the project files.

By default, unity-created Javascript files contain two functions: `Start` and `Update`. We will initialize the connection to the zombie's animator controller in the **Start** function.

6. Within the curly brackets of the `Start` function, add the following line of code:

```
thisAnimator = GetComponent(Animator);
```

Because this code is in `Start`, as soon as the script runs, it will gain access to the animator component and store this in the `thisAnimator` variable for future use.

Next, we will add some code to the `Update` function. Unlike `Start`, which runs only once, when the script is first activated, `Update` runs every frame, so it is usually the best place to check for input.

7. Add the following code within the curly brackets of the `Update` function:

```
if(Input.GetButton("Fire1"))
{
    thisAnimator.SetTrigger("Hits");
}
```

In the first line of code, we check for input from the `Fire1` button (set up by default for the left-mouse button). When this condition is met, we trigger the `Hits` parameter inside the animator controller, enabling the transition to the **Hit** state and playing the `zombie_hit` animation.

8. Save the script in MonoDevelop by navigating to **File | Save**.

If any errors appear in the console, be careful that you have not left out any semicolons (that should end all operations and variables) or curly brackets (that should start and end all functions and statements).

 If you are including any comments for your own references, make sure that single-line comments are preceded with two forward slashes // and block comments are encapsulated by /* and */.

This is a pretty short, simple script. We will be elaborating on this later in the book.

We need to add the script to the zombie character. This can be done by dragging the script from the **Project** panel onto the `zombie_m` game object in the **Hierarchy** panel to attach it as a component.

Next, we will make a few small adjustments to the scene, to make it easier to view our animation.

Adjusting the scene elements to preview the animation

Changing the position and orientation of the camera will make it easier to view the zombie's animation:

1. In the **Hierarchy** panel, select the default **Main Camera** and move it to a position where it is pointing at the zombie.

 A quick way to set the position of the camera in the scene is by performing the following steps:

1. Navigate the **Scene** view so that a chosen object is framed.
2. Select the **Main Camera** game object by clicking on it in the Hierarchy panel.
3. In the menu bar, navigate to **GameObject | Align with View**.

 The camera will be repositioned to match the current **Scene** view navigation.

2. Add a plane to represent the ground in the scene by navigating to **GameObject | Create Other | Plane**.

    The plane should be centered to the scene by default.

    The directional light that is already in the scene should be sufficient to light the character.

3. If necessary rotate the light so that the character is clearly lit.

The light should clearly illuminate the character's face in the scene.

Previewing the hit animation in the game view

Now that we can clearly see the character within the view, we can test the animation:

1. Press the **Play** button in the top-center of the Unity interface.

    The zombie will cycle through its `idle` animation.

2. Click on the left-mouse button.

This will cause the `hit` animation to play once before transitioning back to the **Idle** state.

Summary

In this chapter, we covered the major steps involved in animating a premade character using the Mecanim system in Unity.

We started with FBX import settings for the model and the rig.

Then we covered the creation of the Avatar by defining the bones in the **Avatar Definition** settings.

After that we created a simple example of an animator controller, added it to the character, and added some prepared motion clips.

Finally, we got our male zombie character up and attacking, by writing and implementing a simple control script.

In the next chapter, we will demonstrate the process of rigging a character in 3ds Max and Maya for use in Unity and Mecanim. This time we will start with the male zombie's female counterpart.

2
Rigging Characters for Unity in 3ds Max and Maya

We have already got into some of the major character animation tools that Unity has to offer, but if you have experience modeling and a character that you would like to bring into Unity, this chapter will explain how to get your model rigged and ready.

We will cover typical rigging workflows for 3ds Max and Maya, and illuminate a couple of the pitfalls that you may run into along the way.

We will cover:

- Basic rigging objectives
- Rigging with Biped in 3ds Max
- Rigging with joints in Maya
- Exporting in Unity compatible formats

Understanding the need for rigging

The rigging portion of the character animation process is essential to ready the character to be animated. When rigged, a character will have defined joints, which will allow it to articulate in a realistic way.

A key difference between rigging for a game engine like Unity and rigging for a non real-time animation is that we do not need to set up full character controls in our 3D software.

On export, controls and other helpers will typically be deleted leaving just the mesh, bones, and animation (if there is any). This makes rigging a model for Unity a little easier.

Minimum requirements

As we mentioned briefly in *Chapter 1, The Zombie Attacks!*, there are certain requirements that we need to consider if we want to create a rigged character that is fully compatible with Mecanim's tools. In order to make use of the **Humanoid Avatar** preset in Mecanim, we need a minimum of 15 bones, typically:

* Hips or root joint
* Spine1
* Spine2
* Neck
* Head
* Thigh_R
* Calf_R
* Foot_R
* Thigh_L
* Calf_L
* Foot_L
* UpperArm_R
* ForeArm_R
* UpperArm_L
* ForeArm_L

The skeletons that we will create in 3ds Max and Maya will have quite a few more bones than these—supporting full hand articulation, but this is not strictly necessary to make use of the animation and retargeting tools that Mecanim offers.

Your bones do not have to be named this way, though it is a good idea to adopt consistent naming conventions between your characters. The Avatar in Mecanim acts as an intermediary between the animation and the skeleton, which helps when retargeting animations between different characters.

Mecanim has support for hands, fingers, extra spine links, and a few other bones. The rigs we will set up will exceed the minimum requirement of bones in order to accommodate more detailed animations. We will explore the possibilities of using additional bones later in the project.

Sourcing models

If you are not a modeler, suitable characters are easy to find in the **Unity Asset Store** and other commercial sites. It is possible to find rigged models without having to pay a lot of money, but if you are planning on using them in a commercial project, always check the licensing—typically a small word or text file is included in the zipped folder when you download a model.

The models used in this book are provided by Atelier Sphynx, more are available in the Unity Asset Store at `https://www.assetstore.unity3d.com`.

Modeling for animation

Though an explanation of the full modeling process is beyond the scope of this book, there are a few considerations that you need to be aware of if you have a model that you want to rig for use in Unity:

- **Polycount**: Think about how many times the model is likely to be shown on screen and how big it will be. Typically, characters that are only present in the background or those that are repeated multiple times, would contain less polygons to free up system resources, and maintain a consistent frame rate. The polycount is the amount of triangles, which the character is made up of. This can often be kept to a minimum by deleting unseen parts of a model and reducing the complexity of less important areas.

- **Mesh density**: In order to maintain the semblance of a smooth, continuous surface, modelers often organize their character's topology by the direction and flow of edges. A ring of edges is called an **Edge Loop**. Typically, more edge loops will be necessary on the parts of the mesh that deform. Shoulders, knees, and elbows need to be reinforced to support the deformation caused by joints. Similarly, areas that do not bend or deform can have less edge loops, as the mesh only needs to support the static shape.

- **Quads and triangles**: The 3D applications (including game engines such as Unity) render triangles. Most modeling workflows use quadrangles (or quads), which subdivide more evenly and are easier to UV map and animate. If your model contains anything other than quads or triangles, such as pentagons or hexagons or higher (generally termed **ngons**), you will risk unpredictable results when you try to rig and animate. It is advised to stick to triangles and quads when you are modeling your characters.

Rigging in 3ds Max

In this section, we will demonstrate the rigging process in 3ds Max using Biped.

Biped is a set of tools developed as part of the character studio in 3ds Max and is basically a prefabricated skeleton that can be fully adjusted to fit most bipedal (and also some quadrupedal characters). The main advantage of using this is speed. It will enable you to create a usable character skeleton in a very short span of time. Biped also has **inverse kinematics (IK)** by default. IK can be set up from scratch using the max bones system, but it takes quite a bit more time.

Setting up the scene

Before we get to work, there are a few things we need to do to prepare for rigging:

1. Download the project files from the Packt website if you have not already done so.

2. Start 3ds Max.

3. Set the units to meters by navigating to **Customize | Units Setup**.

4. When the **Units Setup** window appears in the max interface, click on the **Metric** radio button near the top of the **Display Unit Scale** group.

5. Choose **Meters** from the drop-down list.

6. Click on **OK** to save the changes and close the window.

    Next, we will adjust the **Home Grid** size to show meters, which is the unit used in Unity.

7. Right-click on **Snaps Toggle**. This is the button in the top center of the 3ds Max interface, which contains the image of a magnet with the number **2**, **2.5**, or **3**. This will open up the **Grid** and **Snap Settings** window.

8. Click on the **Home Grid** tab.

9. In the **Grid Spacing** field, within the **Grid Dimensions** group, type 1.0 m. This will create major grid lines at one meter intervals.

10. Close the **Grid** and **Snap Settings** window.

Now that we have prepared 3ds Max, we can import the character model into the scene.

Importing the character model

The character model is a female counterpart to the zombie character we animated in *Chapter 1, The Zombie Attacks!*. It has been saved in the **Wavefront OBJ** format, one of the more widely used 3D mesh formats. Our next step is to import the model:

1. Click on the 3ds Max icon in the top-left corner of the 3ds Max interface.

2. Click on **Import** from the drop-down command list.

3. In the **Select File to Import** dialog that appears, navigate to the project files and double-click on the Rigging_Assets folder.

4. Double-click on the Models subfolder, and then the zombie_f subfolder to view its contents.

5. Select the zombie_f.obj file and click on **Open** to close the import dialog.

6. The **OBJ File Import Options** window will appear.

7. Near the bottom of the window, choose **None** as the Preset. Leave all of the other settings at their default values.

8. Click on **Import** to close the window and import the model.

The female zombie character model should appear in your quad viewports. The character is approximately the same polycount the male zombie. It has textures applied and is ready to be rigged:

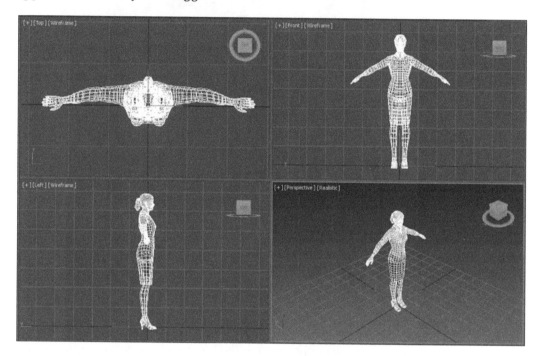

Creating the Biped system

Biped is a customizable character skeleton that can accommodate most two-legged and two-armed characters. It is often used as a quick method for getting character models ready to animate. In this section, we will add and configure the Biped system for use with our character model:

1. Maximize the **Perspective** viewport by right-clicking within the viewport to select it, and then clicking on the **Maximize Viewport Toggle** in the lower-right corner of the max interface.

2. Click on the **Create** tab on the command panel (located on the right side of the interface).

3. From the sub menu, select the **Systems** tab on the far right.

4. Click on the **Biped** button and drag out the Biped rig onto the grid.

Rather than trying to match the full height of the character, try to line up the shoulder joints with the shoulders of the character mesh.

Adjusting the Biped's parameters

Before deselecting the Biped system, adjust the parameters in the **Modify** panel (the icon next to that for the **Create** panel), we need to change a few more parameters in command panel:

1. Change **Body Type** to **Female**. This will change the skeleton to one that better matches the female physiology.

2. Change **Root Name** to zombie_f_, this name will add this as a prefix to all of the bones in the new skeleton, making them easier to identify.

3. Adjust the bone parameters to match the following illustration:

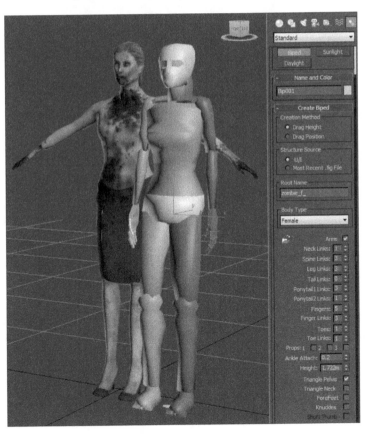

This will give you the right number of bones for the character rig.

Do not worry about the **Twist Links** and **Xtras** parameters at the bottom — these are advanced options that are not necessary for this character.

Next, we will adjust the size and rotation of the individual bones to better match our female zombie.

Adjusting the Biped to fit the character

As a prefabricated rig, Biped is designed to be adapted to various character types. We can scale and rotate all of the bones to fit our character's design:

1. Click on the **Motion** tab in command panel and then activate **Figure Mode** by clicking on the figure icon under the **Biped** rollout. This will allow you to edit the scale and rotation of individual bones:

   Importantly, we need to make sure that the root bone is centered to the world.

2. Click on the **Select By Name** icon in the main tool bar or use the *H* key.

3. Select the zombie_f_ bone from the list and click on **OK** to close the **Select By Name** window.

4. In command panel, rename the bone zombie_f_root by typing this in the **Name** field.

5. Activate the **Select and Move** tool (or press *W* key) and zero out the **X** and **Z** fields in the bottom center of the screen by selecting the number in the field and typing 0.

This will ensure that the skeleton is lined up accurately with the model and help you rig the character effectively using the symmetry shortcuts that Biped offers.

Switching to X-ray mode and freezing the character mesh

To make it easier to see the bones underneath your model, you can use X-ray mode:

1. With the **Select Object** tool active, click on the zombie_f mesh in the viewport.

2. Press *Alt* + *X* to display the current selection in X-ray, making it semi-transparent

   If you now freeze the selection, you can make sure the character mesh does not accidentally get selected during the rigging process.

3. Right-click on anywhere in the viewport and choose **Freeze Selection** from the **Display** menu:

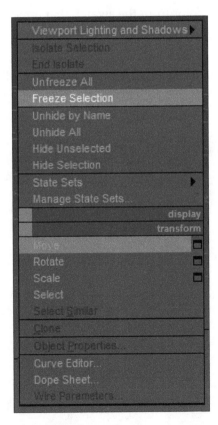

The selected character mesh will become grayed-out, indicating that it is now frozen, though you should still be able to see the Biped bones clearly through the mesh because it is set to X-ray.

You can unfreeze frozen objects at any time by right-clicking on and choosing **Unfreeze All** from the **Selection** menu.

Changing bone display colors

By default, all three of the spine bones that were created are displayed in the same color. To make it easier to differentiate them, the colors should be changed:

1. In the perspective viewport, select `zombie_f_Spine1`.

2. Change the display color by clicking on the colored square in the right of command panel (it will be displayed if you have the **Modify**, **Hierarchy**, or **Motion** tabs active).

3. Choose a different color from the swatch that appears.

4. Repeat this process for `zombie_f_Spine2`.

 The colors that you assign to individual bones will help you to differentiate them in the viewport—the skeleton will never be visible in the game.

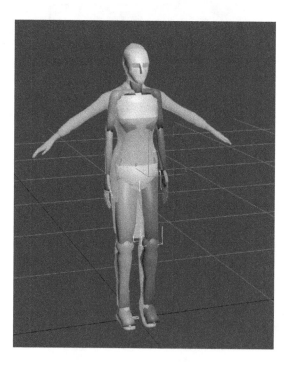

Scaling and orienting the bones to match the character model

The next part of the process will be unique to the character that you are rigging. Follow these steps to adjust the bones to align with the character:

1. Activate the **Select and Scale** tool (or press the *R* key).

2. Set **Reference Coordinate System**, the white drop-down list in the top, center-middle of the interface, from View to Local. This will ensure that the rotation and scale gizmos used to modify the bone are aligned to the bone. This will make it easier to adjust them:

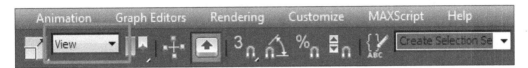

 The Reference Coordinate System is specific to the tool that you are using, so you will have to set it to Local for the **Select** and **Rotate** tool as well.

Scale each of the spine bones to better approximate the proportions of the character's torso:

1. Start by scaling zombie_f_Spine.

2. Continue with the next two spine bones.

3. Scale and rotate the zombie_f_Neck joint.

4. Repeat this process for the head. Try to scale the head bone so that the approximate eye position indicated by the Biped head joint line up with that of the character mesh.

 When you are scaling and rotating bones, try to follow the hierarchical order of the skeleton, so that the bones closest to the root are adjusted first. This will reduce the possibility of changing the size and orientation of bones that you previously adjusted.

The core of the character skeleton should be a pretty good fit before we move on to the peripheral joints and the limbs.

Repositioning the joints for the ponytail and jaw

We created the Biped with two chains of ponytail links. The first set will be used for the character's hair, and the second, which is a single joint, will be used for the character's jaw animation:

1. Activate the **Select and Move** tool (or press the *W* key).

2. Select `zombie_f_Ponytail1` and move it to the area in the back of the character's head where the ponytail starts.

3. Switch to the **Select and Scale** tool (or press the *R* key), scale the joint down so it fits neatly inside of the mesh.

4. Select the next joint in the chain and rotate and scale the joint down until it terminates at the widest part of the ponytail.

5. The last joint should be rotated and scaled so that it reaches the end of the ponytail portion of the character mesh.

6. For the jaw, select a single-joint ponytail chain in the viewport or from the **Select by Name** list.

7. Rename it `zombie_f_Jaw`.

8. Reposition the joint so that it starts just beneath the ear in the **Right** or **Left** viewport.

9. Rotate and scale the joint so that it reaches the character's chin.

The result should appear similar to the following illustration:

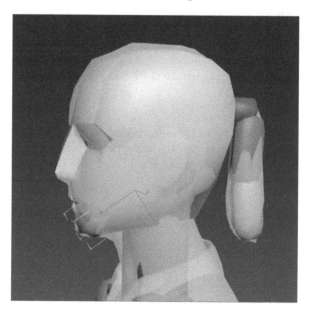

Ponytail links can be moved to any position on the head and used to support anything else that needs to animate such as a nose, hat, jaw, or antennae.

Do not worry about scaling the bones to exactly fit the character mesh, if they poke through the surface in places this is fine. It is more important that you place the joints correctly within the mesh, as individual vertices will be influenced by the bones' respective rotations.

Adjusting limb positions

Assuming that your character is symmetrical like this one, you will only need to rotate and scale the bones on one side of the character.

Bones are color coded. The character's right-side bones are displayed in green and the left-side bones are displayed in blue.

1. Adjust the bones of the left arm, starting with `zombie_f_L_UpperArm`.

2. Move down through the hierarchy to correct the scale and rotation of the lower arm, hand, and finger bones making sure that the joints fit appropriately within the mesh.

3. Repeat this process for the bones of the left leg, starting with `zombie_f_L_Thigh`.

   In the Biped system, certain bones such as the neck and finger roots can also be moved allowing greater flexibility.

4. Switch to the **Select and Move** tool and drag the finger root joints into the correct positions indicated by the character model.

 Lining up the finger and toe bones can be tricky. Hopefully you will be working with a character in which these joints will be suggested in the modeling. Often, characters are created with this in mind – knee, elbow, and finger joints will be slightly bent to facilitate faster and more accurate rigging.

Rather than having to repeat this process for the character's right side, we will be making use of some of Biped's additional features to copy and paste scale and rotation data from one side to the other. First, we need to take care of a few issues with the bone names.

As you are rotating and scaling the finger joints, it should become evident that these joints are identified by number only. It would be more useful if they were given unique names before we get too much further with the rigging process.

Renaming bones

Renaming bones will allow them to be selected more easily in a list, for situations when it is difficult to select them in a viewport. We will assign the finger bones unique names:

1. In the viewport, select the first bone in the left index finger.

2. In the **Modify** panel, rename it `zombie_f_L Index1`.

3. Select the second bone in the index finger, and name it `zombie_f_L Index2`.

4. Continue this process to rename the remaining joint and assign the appropriate names to the bones of the **Middle**, **Ring**, **Little**, and **Thumb** of both hand.

5. Select the left toe bone `zombie_f_L Toe0` and remove the number `0` from the end of the name. Repeat this with the right toe bone.

Now that we made our bone names consistent, we will copy the rotation and scale data from the left side to the right.

Copying and pasting the position, rotation, and scale data from one side to the other

One of the benefits of using the Biped system is that it includes various shortcuts to speed up the rigging process, especially when working with a symmetrical character:

1. Activate the **Select Object tool** (or press the *Q* key) and reselect all of the left side limb bones by dragging a marquee around them within the viewport. Alternatively, you can use the **Select By Name** tool (or press the *H* key).

2. In the command panel, select the **Motion** tab.

3. Scroll down to locate the **Copy/Paste** rollout and make sure that the **Posture** button is activated:

4. Click on the **Create Collection** button. This stores the group of the bones that you selected.

5. Click on the **Copy Posture** button.

6. Click on the **Paste Posture Opposite** button.

The scaling and rotation of the limb should be transferred correctly to the other side.

If there is any offset resulting in the bones not fitting within the mesh on the pasted side, check that the root bone and the character mesh have both been centered to the world and try again:

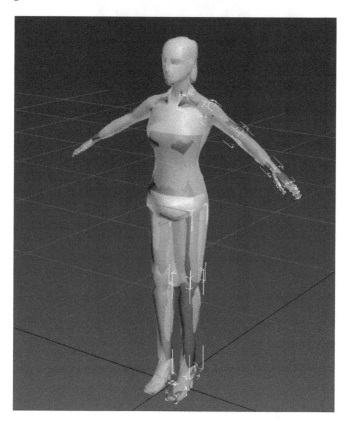

Once the individual bone orientations have been set, the next stage of the rigging process will involve creating a relationship between the character mesh and its skeleton. This is referred to as the **skinning** process.

Skinning the character using the skin modifier

At the time of writing, the best tool to set up the relationship between the character model and the skeleton in 3ds Max is the **Skin** modifier. We will be adding this to the modifier stack and configuring it to work with our skeleton in this step:

1. Select the character model in the viewport.
2. In the **Modify** panel, click on the small arrow next to **Modifier List** to expand the list.

3. Navigate to the **Object | Space Modifiers** section and choose **Skin**.

   The **Skin** modifier will be added to the character model's modifier stack. The modifier's **Parameters** rollout will appear lower down in the **Modify** panel.

   Within the **Parameters** rollout, the **Bones** group contains a list of the bones currently used in the **Skin** modifier. This is empty by default.

4. Click on the **Add** button.

   The **Select Bones** window will appear. This is essentially the same as the **Select by Name** tool that we used previously.

5. In the **Selection Set** option, at the top of the window, click on the arrow and select `zombie_skeleton` from the drop-down list.

6. Holding *Ctrl*, click on `zombie_f_Root` and `zombie_f_Footsteps` at the top of the list to deselect them.

   We are deselecting these two items. The root bone is used to move the whole rig around and does not directly influence any vertices. The footsteps object is used in the creation of walk cycles and is not really a bone.

7. Click on the **Select** button at the bottom of the **Select Bones** window.

   The window will close, and the selected bones will be displayed in the skin modifier's **Bones** list:

The scrollbar on the right of the list will allow you to view all of the selected bones.

8. We need to see the bones to animate them, so if you have hidden them, you can unhide them by right-clicking on and selecting **Unhide by Name** from the **Display** menu.

Before we start rotating the bones, we will make a selection set, which will help us to quickly reselect the bones that make up the skeleton.

Creating a selection set

In 3ds Max, a **selection set** is a stored group of objects or subobjects that can be stored and then quickly accessed via the **Named Selection Sets** box. Using selection sets during animation can save you a lot of time, because you will not have to manually select all of the bones, which make up the skeleton repetitively:

1. Select all the bones in the skeleton using the **Select By Name** tool.
2. Locate the **Named Selection Sets** box just below the main toolbar in the top center of the max interface.
3. Click on once in the field and type zombie_skeleton to name the set.
4. Tap *Enter* to confirm the creation of the new selection set.

The selection set is now stored.

You can now quickly select all of the bones at once by choosing zombie_skeleton from the drop-down list accessed by the small arrow.

 When you choose a selection set containing items which are hidden or frozen, you will be given the option to unhide and unfreeze. This is quicker than having to select all of the objects from the **Unhide by Name** dialog.

Saving the default pose

Before we start rotating any bones, we will save the default bone orientation and position, to make it easier to return to if we accidentally overwrite the initial pose:

1. Reselect the root bone zombie_f_Root.
2. Exit the figure mode by clicking on the **Figure** icon in the **Motion** panel.
3. Click on to select the **Pose** tab in the **Copy/Paste** rollout.
4. Click on the **Copy Pose** icon, and in the **Copied Poses** field, rename it as default.

You should see a thumbnail image of the pose appear in the **Copied Poses** preview panel:

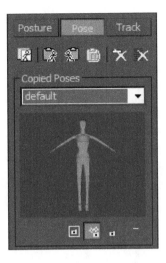

The default pose will now be saved to the collection.

Creating the test pose

The test pose that we create is used to check the quality of the joint deformations. Rather than spending a great deal of time creating an interesting or balanced pose, we are primarily testing the character skinning.

As the character will be required to use a number of different animation sequences in a game, it makes sense to try out different joint rotations. Therefore, the most appropriate kind of pose to test with is an asymmetrical pose such as a walking stance.

We can start by hiding the character model:

1. Select the character in the viewport by clicking on it.
2. Right-click on and choose **Hide Selected** from the **Display** menu.

   This will make it easier to select and adjust individual bones.
3. At the bottom of the main interface, drag the **Track Bar** to frame **30**. This is where we will key the pose.
4. Back in the **Motion** panel, expand the **Key Info** rollout.
5. Start rotating the bones to create the pose. Start with the spine bones.

6. Each time you pose a bone, click on the red **Set Key** button.

    When you set a key, a dark square will appear in the frames position on the track bar to indicate that there is animation data associated with the currently selected joint.

> If you make a mistake, you can click on the **Delete Key** button which will reset the rotation or position of the currently selected bone. The square defining the frame on the track bar will also disappear.

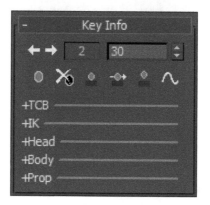

> If you forget to set the key when you have rotated a bone, your changes will be lost when you move the track bar or deselect the bone.
>
> You can reset all of the bones by choosing the **zombie skeleton** selection set from the drop-down at the top of the interface, and then clicking on **Delete Key**.

The Biped skeleton is set up with **Inverse Kinematics (IK)**, so rather than having to adjust each of the bones down through the hierarchy, you can select the hands and feet and move them to a precise position.

Creating a test pose is much quicker and easier using this method. It is also useful for creating interactions, such as foot contacts.

In some situations, you will also want to use **Forward Kinematics (FK)**, which is the strictly hierarchical positioning of joints. Parent joints, such as the clavicle, upper arm, and forearm are rotated in order to position the hand.

With Biped, you can use a mixture of IK and FK to create your test pose:

- ○ Make sure not to forget the extra bones we added for the ponytail and jaw
- ○ The bones for at least one of the hands should also be posed

When all of the bones have been posed and keyframed, we will store the test pose as we did with the `default` pose:

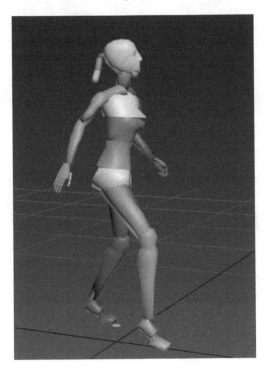

7. Copy the pose and rename it in the same way you did for the `default` pose. Name it `testPose01`.

   The pose has now been saved to the **Collection**, and can be applied to the character whenever it is needed.

8. Unhide the character by right-clicking on and selecting **Unhide By Name** from the **Display** menu.

9. Choose the `female_zombie` object from the list.

10. If X-ray mode is active, switch it off by pressing *Alt + X*.

11. Look closely at the joints — shoulders, elbows, hips, and knees — to make sure that the surface of the mesh deforms smoothly.

Hiding the Biped bones will make it easier to see the deformation of the model:

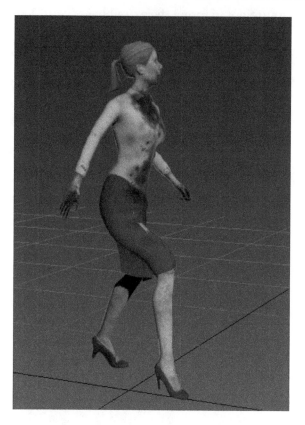

There should be some smooth deformation in these areas, probably a few problems too. We can correct these when we adjust the envelopes in the next step.

Making adjustments to the Skin modifier

The **Skin** modifier does a reasonably good job at setting up smooth deformations between most of the bones. There are some areas such as the head, torso, and feet, which need further adjustment.

When initiated, the **Skin** modifier creates envelopes for each of the bones added to the list. These envelopes can be adjusted by changing their size and position relative to the bones. We can also adjust the influence on individual vertices.

We will start by taking a look at the envelope adjustment.

Adjusting envelopes

In the **Skin** modifier, the **Envelope** is a grouping of vertices influenced by a specific bone. Adjustments to a character's skinning should usually start with these. Envelopes enable broad changes to be quickly made to the skin by adjusting a gizmo capsule rather than adjusting vertices one at a time:

1. Under the **Modify** panel, click on the **+** symbol next to the **Skin** modifier to expand its sub-object levels.

2. Select **Envelope**.

3. In the **Bones** list, lower down in the panel and select `zombie_f_Spine2`.

    The bone's envelope gizmos will appear and a color gradient will be projected on top of the character's texture:

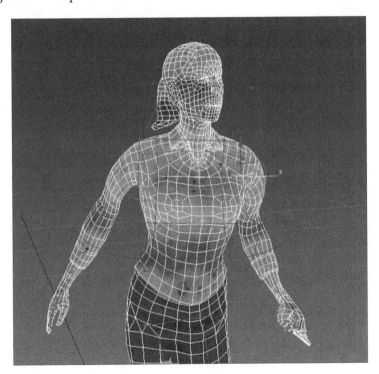

The selected bone's influence is displayed in color temperature, with the strongest influence displayed in red, the least influence is displayed in blue.

The two capsule shaped gizmos define this influence on the vertices. The distance between these two capsules defines how smooth the deformation is.

With the default settings, the character's upper arms appear to be squeezed and pushed too far from the torso.

4. Activate the **Select and Move** tool and drag on one of the control points of the larger capsule.

    The gizmo will rescale as the control point is dragged, resulting in a change in the vertices which are influenced. You will see the gradient change to reflect this.

    The rings that define the size of the envelopes are called **cross sections**. There are two of these for each outer and inner envelope.

5. Reduce the size of the outer envelope to include only the vertices in the upper part of the torso:

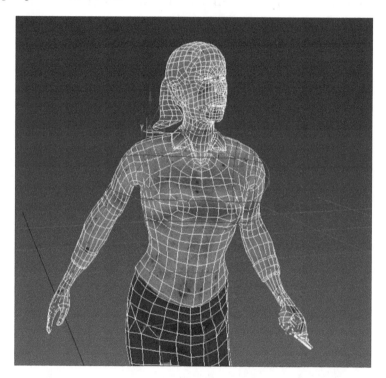

Dragging the control points of the cross sections only allows the rescaling of envelope on one axis. The envelopes can also be shortened and lengthened by moving the two control points connected by the yellow line in the center of the envelope.

These control points can also be moved around to change the actual position of the envelope and therefore the influence of the bone can be offset from the bone's actual position.

Select the core control points one at a time, and move them in toward the center of the character until the shoulders of the character are no longer contained within the inner envelope:

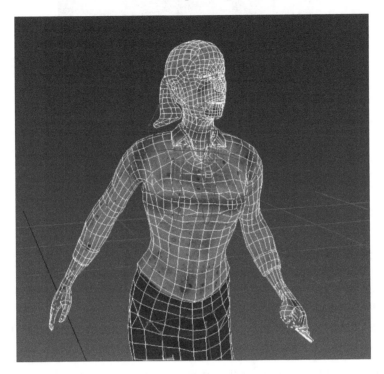

The character's arms should appear fuller and more cylindrical, as they are receiving less influence from the upper spine bone.

6. Select other spine, arm, and leg bones from the list and adjust the envelopes to include just the vertices that you wish the selected bone to influence.

Sometimes the character model's form is complex enough to demand a closer level of adjustment. We will demonstrate this with the head.

Adjusting influence on the head vertices

The vertices in the head are currently influenced by the head, neck, jaw, and ponytail bones, so the results will be pretty messy. Most of the vertices in the head should not deform, so this area requires a different technique to skin successfully:

1. Maximize the **Left** viewport.
2. Return the **Track Bar** to **Frame 0**.

3. Select the `zombie_f_Head` bone from the list in the **Modify** panel:

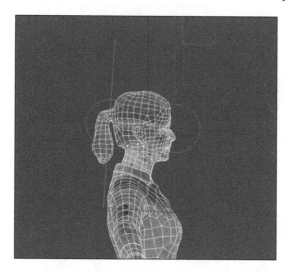

The head envelope is displayed as a capsule gizmo arranged horizontally from front to back. The inner envelope currently includes most of the upper face. The outer envelope includes the whole head and some of the upper torso.

We will start by reorienting and rescaling the envelope to better fit the head and reduce the influence on the vertices of the torso.

4. Select one of the core control points within the head envelope and position it at the top of the ear and level with the eye.

5. Select the other core control point and move it below the ear and level with the lower lip.

6. Drag the inner envelope control points to rescale the envelope to include all of the vertices of the head.

Make sure to include the nose, but do not try to include the ponytail or chin as these will fall under the influence of other bones.

7. Rescale the head's outer envelope by dragging the control points.

    The outer envelope should be only slightly bigger than the inner envelope resulting in a very steep blend between the bone influences:

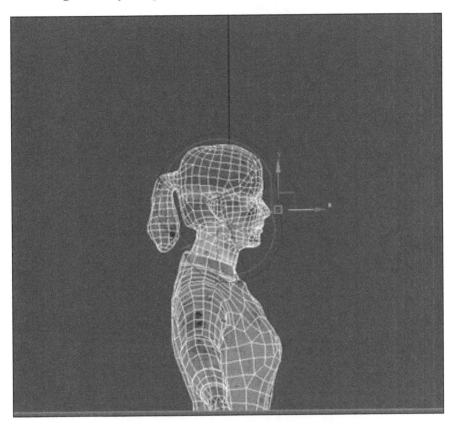

    At this point, we removed the head's influence from the adjacent areas of the character. We need to do some finer work with the jaw to get it to influence the right vertices.

8. Select zombie_f_Jaw from the **Bones** list in the **Modify** panel.

9. Use the control points to rescale the jaw's envelope to influence only the vertices in the lower jaw area.

   This time, we want to leave some space between the outer and inner envelopes so that the deformation is smooth.

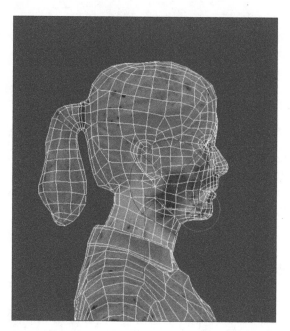

10. Maximize the **Perspective** viewport and slide the track bar to frame 30 to view the results:

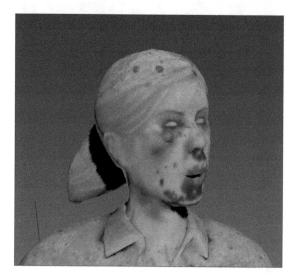

The deformation in the cheeks is smooth as we would expect, but the jaw bone's envelope is influencing too many of the vertices in the upper lip causing it to be stretched.

Beneath the chin, not enough vertices are being influenced as the envelope falls off too sharply. We can fix these problems by painting the skin weights manually.

Painting skin weights for the jaw bone

There are certain situations for a character where we have a mixture of hard (rigid) and soft (deformable) surfaces exceed what we can achieve with skin envelopes on their own. The **Paint Weights** tool in Max allows us to paint bone influence directly onto the mesh:

1. With `zombie_f_Jaw` still selected in the **Bones** list, scroll down to the **Weight Properties** group in the **Modify** panel.

2. Click on the **Painter Options** button:

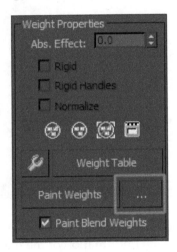

   The **Painter Options** window will appear over the main interface. This is where we will set the size and strength of the weighting brush.

3. In the viewport, make sure you have a clear view of the character's jaw area.

4. Back in the **Modify** panel, uncheck the **Paint Blend Weights** checkbox.

5. Click on the **Paint Weights** button.

   A gizmo will appear when you move the cursor over the character mesh showing the size of the brush.

6. In the **Painter Options** window, set the **Max. Size** to `0.03m`.

    The painting gizmo will change size to reflect this.

7. Set the **Max. Strength** to `-1.0`.

8. Paint over the character's top lip to remove the influence from the jaw bone.

    The color will disappear from the mesh.

9. Set the **Max. Strength** to `0.25`.

10. Paint the area under the chin to add influence from the jaw bone:

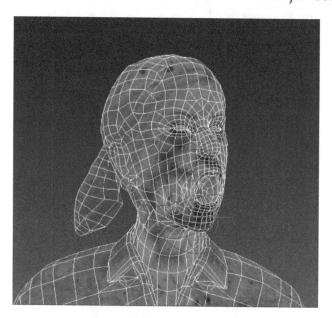

11. Continue painting the skin weights for the back of the neck, hands, feet, and any other areas where the deformation of the mesh needs a tighter definition.

The **Paint Weights** tool will allow you to fine tune each bone's influence on the vertices of the mesh. When the skinning has been completed, we can export the character for use in Unity.

Exporting the rigged character

The final step to complete in 3ds Max is the character export. We will use FBX format, which supports skeletal animation and is recognized by a broad range of software applications including Unity:

1. Uncheck the **Hide Attached Nodes** checkbox to unhide the Biped.

2. Make sure to save your max scene by clicking on the 3ds Max icon in the top-left corner of the interface and choosing **Save As...**

3. Specify a filename and location, and then click on **Save**.

4. Select the skeleton and the character mesh and export it.

5. Click on the **Max** icon and navigate to **Export | Export Selected**.

    In the **FBX Export** window, which appears, there are a few settings that we need to make sure are enabled.

6. In the **Geometry** group, check the boxes next to **Smoothing Groups** and **Triangulate**:

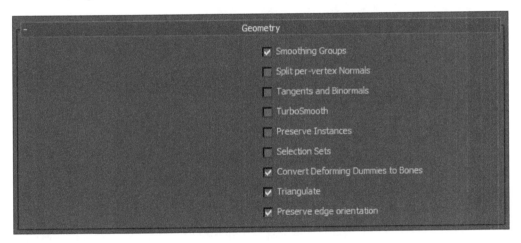

7. We can leave the **Animation** box unchecked, as we no longer need our test pose. The rest of the settings can be left with their default values.

 In the **Embed Media** group, checking the **Embed Media** checkbox is optional, as importing an FBX file with embedded textures will create a textures subfolder within the folder that the model is imported to. You can keep your project more organized by creating your own Textures folder directly within the Assets folder in Unity.

8. Click on to expand the **Advanced Options** rollout.

9. Click on to expand **Units**.

   Our model has been built to scale, but we need to make sure that it is not rescaled in the FBX settings.

10. Uncheck the **Automatic** checkbox.

11. From the **Scene units converted to** drop-down list, select **Meters**. This is the unit of measurement used in Unity:

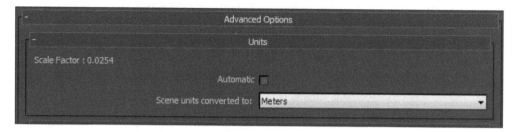

12. Save the FBX file as `zombie_female.FBX`.

The character can now be imported into Unity as detailed in *Chapter 1, The Zombie Attacks!*

The next section details the process of rigging a character model in Maya.

Rigging in Maya

Like 3ds Max, Maya is a major software application used in game asset creation. One of its major advantages is that unlike 3ds Max, it is compatible with Mac operating systems. Its dependence on key combinations rather than point and click icons arguably makes the modeling and rigging process faster.

Though Maya has fewer options for rigging than 3ds Max, its rigging and animation toolset is known for being easy to access and use.

Setting up Maya to rig our character model

Before we import the model and start adding the joints, we will spend a little time setting up Maya to ensure our rigged model is compatible with Unity.

These next steps are optional, but will make for a smoother workflow and more predictable result, particularly if you are working with a sourced model that you did not create yourself.

Setting system units to meters

Unity uses meters as its default unit, so it makes sense to adopt this unit for our rigging work:

1. Start Maya.

2. Open the **Preferences** tab by navigating to **Window | Settings/Preferences | Preferences**.

3. When the window pops up, click on **Settings** in the **Categories** column on the left side of the window.

4. In the **Working Units** group, change **Linear** units to **Meters**.

5. Click on the **Save** button to store the settings.

Changing the display grid size

Typically, the default grid display will not be a good size for work in meters, but this can be easily adjusted:

1. In the main toolbar, click on the box next to **Display – Grid** to open the **Grid Options** window.

2. In the **Gridlines Every** field, type 0.1.

This will divide every meter with 10 gridlines, spaced 10 centimeters apart.

Importing the model

Now that we have got Maya set up, we can import out model, which is formatted as a Wavefront OBJ file. This is one of the more common 3D model formats:

1. Download and unzip the project files from the Packt website if you have not already done so.

2. Import the zombie character model into the new scene by navigating to **File | Import...**

3. In the **Import** window, navigate to the project files.

4. Double-click on the Rigging Assets folder and then the Models subfolder.

5. The female zombie model and texture are in the zombie_f folder.

6. Open the folder and select zombie_f.obj.

7. Click on the **Import** button.

   The character should appear in the main viewport. The model will appear face down, and by default, the **Wireframe** viewport display is enabled.

8. Select the character mesh by clicking on it in the viewport.

9. In **Attribute Editor** on the right side of the Maya interface, select the `zombie_f: zombie_f` node.

10. In the first **Rotate** field, click on and drag to select the value.

11. Enter the value 90 and tap *Enter*.

    The character should now be rotated correctly in the viewport.

12. Activate the **Smooth Shade All** and **Textured** viewport display buttons to make sure that the textures are visible on the character model.

The character should now appear textured within the viewport:

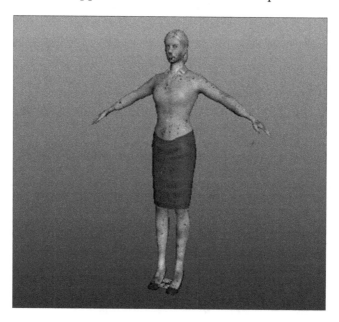

Adjusting the model scale

In terms of real-world scale, we can see that the zombie character model is not the right size for a typical human.

Maya imported the `obj` file at a half scale making the zombie character less than one meter tall! This is something that you need to watch out for when working with sourced models, as different 3D applications read model scale differently.

It is best to fix this issue now, before we start creating the joint hierarchy. We can also fix this issue within Unity, by adjusting the **Scale Factor** option within the **Model Import** settings as demonstrated in *Chapter 1, The Zombie Attacks!*:

1. Click on the **Select Tool** (or press the *Q* key).

2. Select the zombie character's mesh in the viewport.

3. Switch to the **Scale Tool** (or press the *R* key).

4. In the **Channel Box** list on the right side of the Maya interface, locate the **Scale** fields.

5. Type 2.54 into the **Scale X**, **Scale Y**, and **Scale Z** fields to scale the model uniformly.

   The grid lines should show that the zombie character is now around 1.75 meters tall, which is a reasonable height for a human female.

6. Freeze the transform data to store the new scale by navigating to **Modify | Freeze Transformations**.

In the next step, we will optimize the view to make the creation and adjustment of the rig easier.

Adjusting the viewport display and toolset for joint creation

We will switch to an orthographic view to make sure our joints are positioned accurately within the character model:

1. Tap space to activate the **Quad** view.

2. Select the **Front** viewport by right-clicking within it.

3. Tap space once more to maximize the front view.

4. Use the navigations hotkeys to zoom in on the upper half of the character's body. Use *Alt* + right-click onto zoom, *Alt* + middle-click to pan.

5. Switch back to the **Wireframe** viewport display by clicking on the button at the top of the viewport or by tapping *4* on the keyboard.

6. Choose the **Front** viewport, and zoom out far enough that you can see the torso and head of the character.

7. If it is not already active, switch to the **Animation** menu set, by clicking on the small arrow within the rectangular gray box in the top left of the interface:

Now, it is time to start creating the joint hierarchy.

Creating joints for the back, neck, and head

In Maya, the vertices that make up a model are influenced by joints, rather than bones as in 3ds Max. Actually, this distinction doesn't make a lot of difference in the rigging and animation of a character.

The zombie's skeleton will be built using the joint tool:

1. Enable the **Animation** toolset by clicking on the tab near the top middle of the interface.
2. Click on the **Joint Tool** icon from the tool shelf near the top of the interface.
3. Click on the model at the pelvis to create the first joint.
4. Click it to add three more joints for the spine, one for the neck and the other one for the head.
5. When you are finished, exit the joint tool by clicking on the **Select** tool from the main toolbar on the right of the interface.

    By default, the joints are a little too small to be seen clearly in the viewport.

6. Navigate to **Display | Animation | Joint Size**.
7. In the **Joint Display Scale** window, change the scale from 1.00 to 2.00.
8. Tap *Enter* to save the change before closing the window.

You will get the following output:

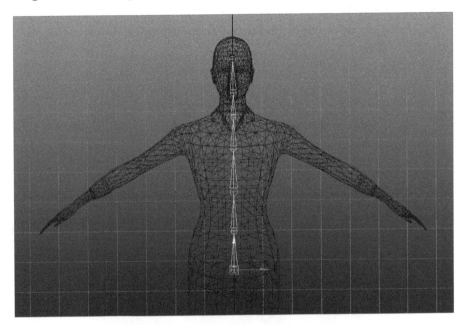

Next, we will implement our joint naming conventions.

Renaming and repositioning the joints

By default, Maya names each joint with a number according to the order in which it was created. Giving them more specific names will make the resulting skeleton much more user friendly:

1. Click on each joint in turn, using **Channel Box** or **Attribute Editor** to rename it:

   ○ **Joint1**: `zombie_f_root`

   ○ **Joint2**: `zombie_f_spine`

   ○ **Joint3**: `zombie_f_spine1`

   ○ **Joint4**: `zombie_f_spine2`

   ○ **Joint5**: `zombie_f_neck`

   ○ **Joint6**: `zombie_f_head`

2. Switch to the **Right** viewport.

3. Activate the **Move** tool.

4. Drag each of the joints into position to follow the curve of the character's spine, starting with `zombie_f_root`.

5. You can cycle down through the hierarchy using the down cursor key:

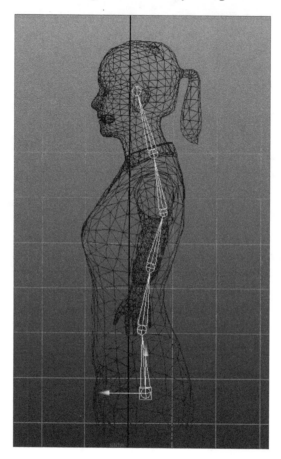

Creating the leg joints

Usually while rigging a symmetrical character like this, we can use the symmetry tools to copy joint chains from one side of the character to the other.

It makes sense to finish naming and positioning each joint before you copy the chain:

1. In the **Right** viewport, activate the **Joint Tool** and create a joint for the upper leg.

2. Create further joints at the knee, ankle, ball of foot, and toe.

3. Rename the joints:
    - ° **Joint1**: `zombie_f_thigh_L`
    - ° **Joint2**: `zombie_f_calf_L`
    - ° **Joint3**: `zombie_f_foot_L`
    - ° **Joint4**: `zombie_f_toe_L`

4. In the **Front** viewport, move the joints to fit within the character mesh:

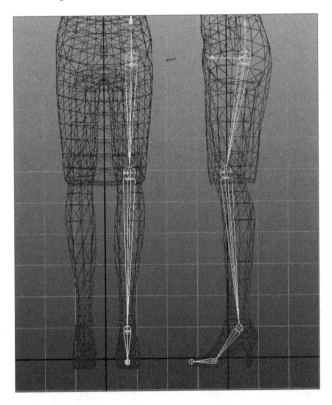

Creating the arm joints

We will start the arm the same way that we created the joint chains for the leg. Because there are so many more joints in the hand, we will switch to using some different techniques to speed up the process:

1. Switch to the **Top** view.
2. Reactivate the **Joint** tool.

3. Create a single joint chain from the shoulder to the end of the index finger, clicking on to create a joint at each juncture.

4. Rename the joints:
   - **Joint1**: zombie_f_arm_L
   - **Joint2**: zombie_f_foreArm_L
   - **Joint3**: zombie_f_hand_L
   - **Joint4**: zombie_f_index_L
   - **Joint5**: zombie_f_index1_L
   - **Joint6**: zombie_f_index2_L
   - **Joint7**: zombie_f_index_NUB

5. Center the **Arm** joint within the shoulder.

6. Position the **foreArm** joint a little further back to make sure the elbow bends correctly.

7. Switch between the **Front, Top, Right,** and **Perspective** viewports to arrange the remaining joints to fit the character mesh:

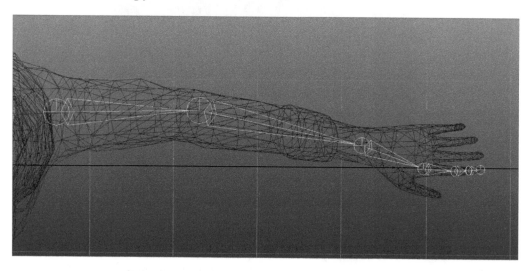

Getting the finger joints to line up correctly can be a little tricky. It helps to orbit around the hand in the perspective view.

Cloning the finger joints

For the remaining thumb and finger joints, you can clone those that you initially created for the index finger:

To do this:

1. Switch to and maximize the **Perspective** viewport.

2. Use the keyboard combination *Alt* + click to navigate the view until you are looking down at the hand.

3. Activate the **Smooth shade all**, **Textured**, and **XRay joints** viewport displays by clicking on the small buttons at the top of the viewport.

    This should make it easier to see the joints within the mesh.

4. Select the joint at the root of the index finger: zombie_f_index.

5. Use the keyboard combination *Ctrl* + *D* to duplicate the joints.

    The whole chain will be duplicated and become selected.

6. Use the **Move** tool to drag the root of the new finger chain so that it fits within the middle finger.

7. Rename the new joints and fine tune their positions before you do the same for the ring finger, little finger, and the thumb.

Positioning these bones one at a time will make this process easier. The result should look like this:

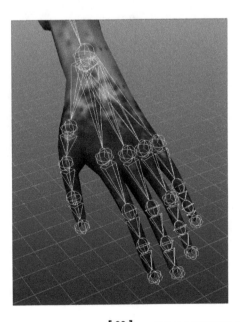

Mirroring joints for the leg and arm chains

The left side of the zombie character's skeleton has been completed – it is a simple task to duplicate the limb joints for the right side:

1. Switch to the **Front** viewport and select zombie_f_thigh_L.

   This will select the whole chain of joints for the left leg.

2. From the menu at the top of the interface, click on the **Skeleton** tab and then the options box next to **Mirror Joint**.

3. In the **Mirror Joint Options** window that appears, set the **Mirror across** axis to **YZ**.

4. In the **Replacement names for duplicated joints** group, enter L in the **Search for:** field and enter R in the **Replace with:** field:

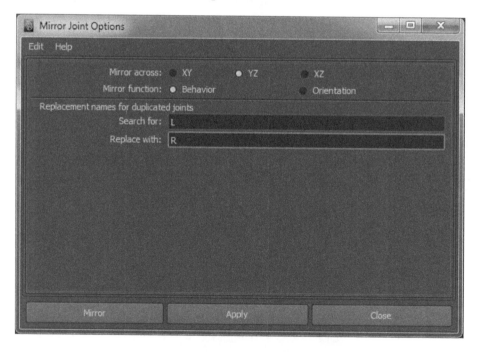

5. Click **Apply**.

   This will recreate the joint chain on the right side of the character.

   Maya will replace the **L** (for left) markers with **R** (for right) in the joint names. However, it is always a good idea to go through and check each joint to make sure that the names are correct.

6. Use the same process to mirror the joints of the left arm.

Next, we will attach the limb joint chains to the spine chain.

Connecting the arm and leg chains

Keeping the limb chains separate from the main body joints is a good idea, while you are tweaking the positions within the character mesh.

Now, it is time to connect them:

1. Activate the **Select Tool** by pressing the *Q* key.
2. Click on `zombie_f_thigh_L`.
3. *Shift* + click on `zombie_f_root` to add it to the selection.
4. From the main toolbar, click on **Skeleton** and then select the options box next to **Connect Joints**.
5. In the **Connect Joint Options** window that pops up, click on the **Parent Joint** radio button.

    The joints will be connected.

6. Repeat this operation for the right leg chain and both arm chains.

It is usually a good idea to wait until the end to add any unique joints. In this case, the character has a ponytail which will be animated. We still need to add a joint for the lower jaw.

Creating the ponytail and jaw joints

These additional joints will be used to add a little character to the animation sequences later in the book. They will be set up quite simply:

1. Switch to the **Right** viewport.
2. Activate the **Joint Tool** and click on `zombie_f_head` (making it the parent).
3. Add a joint at the portion of the mesh where the ponytail is connected to the back of the head.
4. Click within the geometry of the ponytail to create three additional joints. Try to position a joint where the hair starts to turn down, another in the widest part of the tail and the last where it terminates.
5. Click on the **Select Tool** to exit **Joint Tool**.
6. To create the jaw, activate **Joint Tool**.
7. Click on `zombie_f_head`.

8. Create a joint, just beneath the character's ear.

9. Click on near the character's chin to create the second and last jaw joint.

10. Rename the additional joints using **Channel Box** or **Attribute Editor**, being careful to follow the character's naming conventions.

This will result in a skeleton comprised of 69 joints, quite a few more than the minimum required by Mecanim:

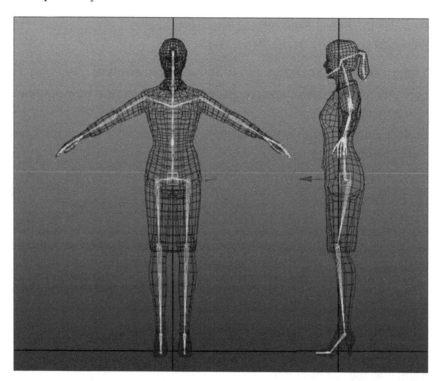

Aligning joint transforms

You may note that when you activate **Rotate Tool**, the rotation axis for some of the joints is pointing in the wrong direction—this will cause a few problems when animating, or even testing the skin binding within Maya:

1. Select `zombie_f_root`.

2. From the menu bar, click on **Skeleton** and then the options box next to **Orient Joint**.

    The **Orient Joint Options** window should appear.

3. Check the boxes for **Orient Joint to World** and **Orient children of selected joints**.

4. Click on **Apply**:

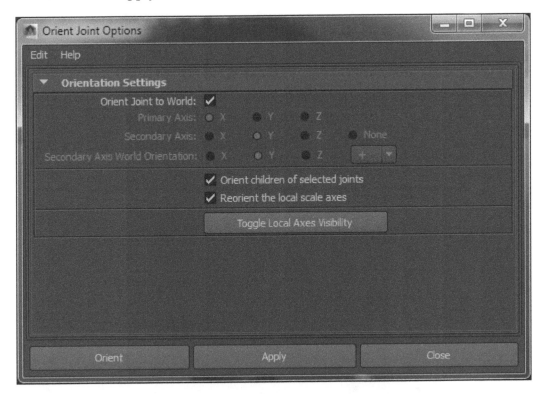

All joints should now face forward. The actual position of the joint chains should remain the same.

Creating a test pose

Now that we have a symmetrical skeleton, we will go through the binding process and test this with a simple pose:

1. Hide the character mesh by selecting it in the viewport and navigating to **Display | Hide | Hide Selection** from the menu bar.

2. Activate the **Auto Keyframe** toggle, by clicking on the key button in the lower-right corner of the Maya interface. It will turn red when enabled.

If the **Auto Keyframe** toggle is not visible in the Maya interface, it can be made visible in the menu bar. Navigate to **Display | UI Elements** and check the box next to **Range Slider**.

3. Make sure **Time Slider** is located at frame 1.

4. Select zombie_f_root in the viewport.

5. Tap *S* on the keyboard to create the first keyframe.

6. Drag the **Time Slider** to frame 10.

7. Rotate zombie_f_root a few degrees to the right or left.

   When you return the Time Slider to its default position at frame 1, the joint should return to its original rotation.

8. Continue this process with the rest of the joints to create a simple test pose:

You can use the down cursor key to navigate down through the hierarchy of joints. This comes in particularly useful when there is a high density of joints like the fingers where selecting individual bones one at a time can be problematic.

Try not to make the pose too extreme. The binding only needs to be good enough to support the typical poses that your character will be in. If you set the bar too high by creating poses which are too gymnastic, you will have a hard time adjusting the skin weights to deform the character's topology in a realistic way.

Binding the character mesh to the skeleton

The binding process involves associating the character mesh with the hierarchy of joints, which make up the skeleton.

For organic-type characters, the smooth bind method is usually the best choice. Using a smooth bind each vertex in the character mesh can receive influence from more than one joint.

Typically, vertices near a joint will receive influence from this joint and the joint's parent in the hierarchy, creating the appearance of smooth bending in an elbow, shoulder, or knee:

1. Unhide the character mesh by navigating to **Display** | **Show** | **All** in the menu bar.
2. Make sure **Time Slider** is located at frame 1.
3. Open the **Outliner** tab and click on `zombie_f_root` to select it.
4. Hold *Shift* and click on the character mesh to add it to the selection.
5. From the menu bar click on **Skin**.
6. Select **Bind Skin** and then click on the options box next to **Smooth Bind**.
7. In the **Smooth Bind Options** window which pops up, change the **Max Influences** to 4 (the maximum allowed by Unity).
8. Click on **Apply**.

Now, when you drag the **Time Slider** to the test pose on frame 10, the character mesh will deform to follow the joints:

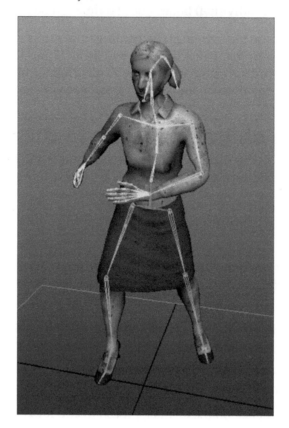

The default settings are a good start, but you will usually need to fine tune these to get a smooth and lifelike result.

Maya will try to blend between the different joint influences, sometimes it will get it wrong. Quite often if the arms are close to the torso, the arm joints may influence the vertices in the torso or vice versa, as is the case here.

With the head of the character, sometimes too much influence is drawn from the neck bone, causing the lower part of the head to become distorted. This can be corrected by painting the skin weights to reduce the influence from the neck joint.

Painting skin weights

To adjust the skin weights:

1. Select the character mesh.

2. Choose the **Wireframe On Shaded** and **Smooth Shade All** viewport display icons from the top of the viewport.

3. From the menu bar, click on **Skin** and then select **Edit Smooth Skin**. Click on the options box next to **Paint Skin Weights Tool**.

4. From the **Tool Settings** dialog that appears, select the joint whose influence you want to edit with the paintbrush cursor that appears in the viewport.

5. Begin painting the mesh to increase the joint's influence.

 You can change the size and softness of the brush and adjust the value as necessary in the **Tool Settings** window.

As you paint the weight for each joint, the mesh will appear white where there is the most influence and black where there is no influence:

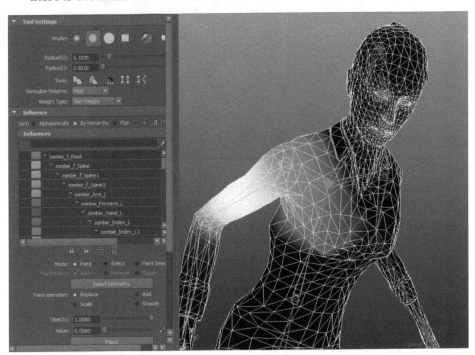

In this case, too much of the character's mesh is being influenced by the arm.

6. We can fix this by lowering the brush **Value** field in the **Skin Weights** window to 0, by dragging it to the left, and then painting over the affected area.

7. We will also need to repaint the weights for the spine joints so that they exert more influence over this area. Set the **Value** field to 1.0, and repaint the areas of the torso for each spine joint:

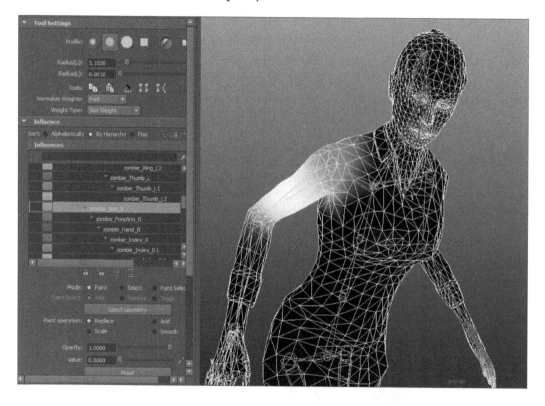

8. Repeat this process for the rest of the character, working from the root joint down through the hierarchy and defining the influence from the parent joints before the child joints.

9. Terminal joints such as the end ponytail and jaw joints, and the last finger joints should not have any influence on the mesh, so assign all of the weight for these areas to the preceding joint.

You may find it necessary to adjust the test pose in order to test the mesh deformation at all of the joints.

When the skin weight adjustments are complete, the last step is to export the skinned character in FBX format.

Exporting for unity

Once we made sure to save our progress, we will clean up the scene a little before exporting for Unity:

1. First, we will delete the history by navigating to **Edit | Delete By Type | History**.

   This will make sure that no unwanted data is exported that may bloat our FBX file and cause problems in Unity.

2. Next, we will show everything within the viewport by navigating to **Display | Show | All**.

3. Select the root joint `zombie_f_root`.

4. Activate **Outliner** by navigating to **Window | Outliner**.

5. When the **Outliner** window opens, *Shift* + click on the **+** symbol next to `zombie_f_root` in the list.

   This will expand the joint hierarchy, allowing you to see all of the joints.

6. Add to the selection by holding *Ctrl* (*Cmd* on a Mac) and clicking on each of the joints in the **Outliner** window. Ignore all terminal joints such as the last numbered joint from each finger, the ponytail, jaw, and the toe joints.

   These joints have no actual influence on the character mesh, so they are redundant and are not needed in Unity.

7. When the remaining joints have been selected, add the character mesh to the selection before closing the **Outliner**.

8. Export the selection by navigating to **File | Export Selection**.

9. When the **Export Selection** window opens, make sure that FBX export is defined in the **Files of type** drop-down list at the bottom of the window.

10. In the **Options** panel on the right of the window, expand the **File Type Specific Options** list.

11. In the **Units** rollout, make sure that **File units converted to** is set to **Centimeters** and the **Automatic** checkbox is unchecked:

12. Leave the remaining parameters at their default settings.

13. Designate a save location by navigating to an appropriate folder in the main area of the window.

 It is not recommended to save FBX files directly to your Unity project. It is usually safer to create a folder somewhere on your hard drive, where you can output your FBX files before dragging them into Unity to import them.

14. Type `zombie_f` into the **File name** field near the bottom of the interface.

15. Click on the **Export Selection** button.

The skinned `zombie_f` character has been exported, and it can be brought into Unity as demonstrated in *Chapter 1, The Zombie Attacks!.*

Summary

In this chapter, we explored character rigging techniques in 3ds Max and Maya.

Starting with the creation of skeletons and the arrangement of bones (or joints) to fit a modeled character mesh, we explored the crucial relationship between the character and its skeleton.

In 3ds Max, we adapted a Biped rig to fit our female zombie character by scaling and rotating the default joints to fit the character's initial pose. We then used the skin modifier to connect the rig to the character model, fine tuning the envelope settings to correct the range of influence from each bone until the character deformed smoothly in the test pose that we created.

Working in Maya, we created a full hierarchy of joints from scratch, by assembling individual chains of joints for the spine, leg, and arm. We implemented workable naming conventions, before mirroring our joint chains to complete the main skeleton. After adding additional joints for the ponytail and jaw, we used smooth bind to define the relationship between the rig and the character model and fine tuned this with the Paint Weights tool until the characters vertices appeared to be appropriately influenced by the joints in our test pose.

At this point, you should be ready to dive into Unity and bring a character to life, exploring environmental interaction in *Chapter 3, Interacting with the Environment.* This time, we will be using the Mecanim tools to set up an initial state machine for our first person character model.

3
Interacting with the Environment

In this chapter we will explore several different kinds of interaction within Unity.

When we focus on the player and environment, interaction is based on a visual response to the player's input, and in a game, this usually takes the form of animation.

In this case, our game is played from a first-person perspective—we will not see the full character on screen, so what the player experiences, needs to concisely convey the state of the game.

Some first-person games display a weapon or just a crosshair. Our game will involve more than just shooting, so we will see the character's hands and arms—this will allow us to demonstrate different kinds of animation within Unity.

Mecanim will allow us to trigger animations according to player input and other conditions—try to think beyond the simple playing of an animation sequence when a button is pushed—Mecanim is capable of more than this and can bring about a richer user experience.

The interactive aspect of the game also necessitates setting up ready made objects called prefabs that our player can collect during the game.

We will cover:

- The player character game object and its components
- First-person camera adjustment
- Adding animation sequences
- Adding a weapon

- Importing, previewing, and implementing animation sequences
- The animator controller – player state machine
- Mecanim-friendly animation scripting
- Creating and using prefabs
- Scripting animation responses for collectables

Working through this chapter will give you an understanding of how player interaction can be achieved and how animation can be used to present the player's connection to the space.

Importing the project assets package

The asset package that you need to follow the chapters of this book is included in the project file. If you have not already downloaded this, you will need to get it from the Packt website.

Once unzipped, you will find the PACKT_CAWM.unitypackage which contains the project hierarchy and sample content and code. After that follow these steps:

1. Launch Unity.
2. Open your Unity project if it does not launch by default, or create a new one if you have not already done so.
3. Import the package by navigating to **Assets | Import Package | Custom Package...**.
4. In the window that appears, navigate to the location where you unzipped the project files and choose **PACKT_CAWM.unitypackage**.
5. In the **Importing Package** dialog that appears over the main interface, make sure that all assets are checked before pressing the **Import** button.

It may take a short time for all of the assets to finish loading.

Setting up the player character

Just like the enemy characters from the previous chapters, the player character has been exported from external software as an FBX file. This file contains the rigged model. The player's material is already set up and will be applied to the model in this section.

The import settings will need to be adjusted and components added before we save the game object as a prefab. From that point, the player character can be instanced in any number of game levels.

Creating a new scene

We will start with a fresh scene so we can set up the character without the distractions of scenery. This can be done by creating a blank scene, using the menu bar and navigating to **File | New Scene**.

In the next step we will be adding the player model.

Adding the player character model to the scene

The player character model has been stored as a **Prefab**, enabling it to be instantiated quickly in any level. The player model's material has already been set up:

1. In the **Project** panel, navigate to the PACKT_Prefabs folder.

2. Locate player_m and drag it into the **Hierarchy** panel to instance it.

   The model only extends as far as the player can see in the first-person camera, though it has a full skeletal rig, allowing us to maintain compatibility with the animation sequences we are using for the zombie characters.

   Our player character is Wayne, the janitor in the office building where the zombie outbreak has taken place. It is his responsibility to "clean up" the mess.

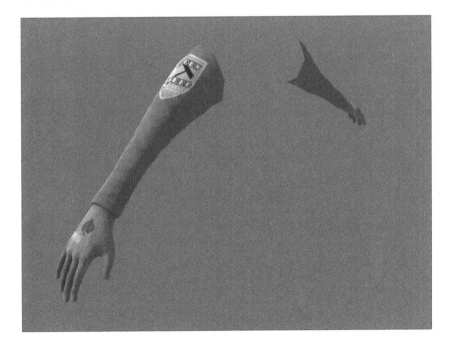

3. Double-click `player_m` within the **Hierarchy** panel to zoom in on the game object.

The next step will get the player character model moving.

Adding the character controller

Unity comes with a prefabricated **First-Person Shooter** (**FPS**) Controller, which will help us get up and running with our player. The FPS Controller is included in the character's controller assets package, which we need to import:

1. Import the character's asset package by navigating to **Assets | Import Package | Characters**.

2. In the **Importing Package** dialogue which appears over the main Unity interface. Check the **None** button at the bottom.

3. Then check the checkboxes next to `Editor`, `FirstPersonCharacter` `CrossPlatFormInput`, and `Utility`.

   All of the associated components will also become checked.

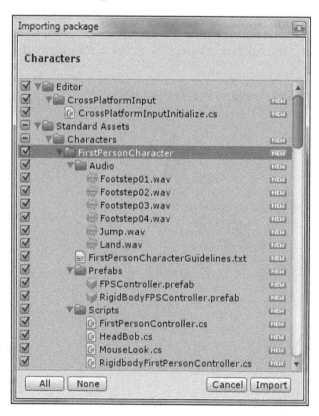

4. Click the **Import** button.

   You may have to wait for a short time while the assets are loaded.

5. In the **Project** panel, expand the `Standard Assets` folder and then the `Character Controllers` subfolder and then finally the `Prefabs` subfolder.

6. Drag the `FPSController.prefab` into the **Scene** view or **Hierarchy** panel.

7. In the **Inspector** panel, zero out the prefab's **Position** coordinates, so it is centered within the world. Do this by typing 0 into the **Position** fields for **X**, **Y**, and **Z**.

   The controller should appear as a capsule shape, with a number of gizmos and a camera icon.

8. In the **Hierarchy** panel select and delete the **Main Camera** object.

   The **Main Camera** is added with a default scene in Unity, and as `FPSController` contains a camera, we no longer need this.

9. If you cannot see the controller within your **Scene** view, click the `FPSController` object twice within the **Hierarchy** panel to zoom in on it.

10. Click the small arrow next to its name to expand its hierarchy.

11. Drag the `player_m` game object onto `FirstPersonCharacter`, making the camera the model's parent.

Next, we will add some basic geometry for the floor so we can test the controller:

1. Add a plane game object by navigating to **Game Object | 3D Object | Plane**.

2. Rename the plane `floorObject`.

3. In the **Inspector** panel, zero out `floorObject` plane's position by entering 0 in the **Position** fields for **X**, **Y**, and **Z**.

4. Set its scale to 5 in the **X** and **Z** fields.

   At this point if we select the `FPSController` game object, we should see its capsule collider intersecting with the `floorObject`.

5. In the **Inspector**, enter 1 in the **Position Y** field to move the `FPSController` up so that it sits on top of the `floorObject`.

We will get the following output:

At this point, the FPSController with its attached camera and player model can be navigated around the empty scene. However, the default pose will not allow us to see any part of the model from the camera view, so we will need to import an animation clip to fine tune the player's position. Before we do this, we will adjust the camera settings a little to better suit our player.

Adjusting the camera height

The FPSController object's child object FirstPersonCharacter contains the camera component that defines the first-person view. By default, this object is positioned around 0.8 meters up from the center of the character controller, which is 1.8 meters high. We want to move this down to eye level, which is more natural and consistent with the height of the enemies and scenery within the game.

We will use a height of 1.67 meters, which is 5'6", a good average eye level for a human. We need to take into account that our camera is already 1 meter off the ground as it is parented to the character controller. In the **Inspector** panel, set `FirstPersonCharacter` object's **Position Y** value to `0.67` to correct the height.

You should see the object move within the **Scene** view. To finalize the adjustment of the `FirstPersonCharacter`, we will add an animation sequence for our character.

Adding the shoot idle animation

The **shoot idle** sequence will show the character in a typical shooting stance, ready to fire.

At the moment, our player does not have an animator controller, which is necessary to preview animation. We will add a temporary controller so we can view the player character model in its `ShootIdle` pose and conclude the camera adjustment:

1. In the **Project** panel, click the `PACKT_Controllers` folder to view its contents in the **Assets** panel.

2. Drag `ch3_1` into `player_m` object's empty **Controller** slot, located within the **Animator** component in the **Inspector** panel.

    The `ch3_1` animator controller will become active in the **Animator** panel.

3. If the **Animator** tab is not visible at the top of the main view panel, activate it from the main menu by navigating to **Window** | **Animator**:

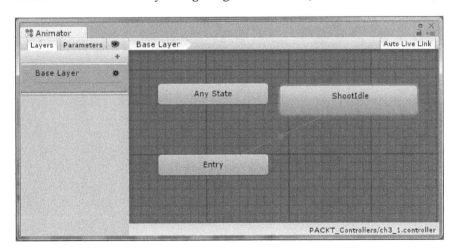

Aside from the defaults **Any State** and **Entry** the controller only contains a single state: **ShootIdle**. This is displayed in orange, indicating that it is the default state and will become active when the scene starts:

4. In the **Animator** panel, click the **ShootIdle** state to view its parameters in the **Inspector** panel. It does not currently contain an animation clip.

5. In the **Project** panel, locate the PACKT_Animations folder.

6. Click it to view its contents in the **Assets** panel.

7. Click the pistol_idle animation folder to view the animation clips contained within it.

8. Drag the pistol_idle animation into the **ShootIdle** state's motion field to add it.

9. Test the game by pressing the **Play** button in the top center of the Unity interface.

   The default camera settings will clip the first-person model a little too much. We can fix this by adjusting the **Clipping Planes** value.

10. Select FirstPersonCharacter in the **Hierarchy** panel.

11. In the **Inspector** panel, locate the **Clipping Planes** values under the **Camera** component.

12. Set the **Near** value to 0.05.

   The player's arms should now extend all the way under the camera without a gap.

Next, we will add the player's gun and fine tune the position coordinates of the player character mesh.

Adding and parenting the gun

The player character's gun has been saved as a **Prefab**. Adding it to the player will allow us to fine tune the model's position in the first-person view:

1. In the **Hierarchy** panel, *Alt* + click the small arrow next to player_m to fully expand its hierarchy.

2. Locate the zombie_m_HandR bone:

```
                    ▼ zombie_m_ThumbL1
                        ▼ zombie_m_ThumbL2
                            zombie_m_ThumbL_Nub
                    zombie_m_WristL
        ▼ zombie_m_ShldrR
            ▼ zombie_m_ArmR
                ▼ zombie_m_ForeArmR
                    ▼ zombie_m_HandR
                        ▼ zombie_m_IndexR
                            ▼ zombie_m_IndexR1
                                ▼ zombie_m_IndexR2
                                    zombie_m_IndexR_Nub
                        ▼ zombie_m_LittleR
                            ▼ zombie_m_LittleR1
                                ▼ zombie_m_LittleR2
                                    zombie_m_LittleR_Nub
                        ▼ zombie_m_MiddleR
                            ▼ zombie_m_MiddleR1
                                ▼ zombie_m_MiddleR2
                                    zombie_m_MiddleR_Nub
```

 You can also type the bone's name into the search field at the top of the **Hierarchy** panel and then select it when it appears in the search list.

3. In the **Project** panel, click the PACKT_Prefabs folder to view its contents in the **Assets** panel.

4. Locate the Gun prefab and drag it into the **Hierarchy** panel to create an instance of it in the scene.

5. Drag it onto the zombie_m_HandR bone in the **Inspector** panel to make it a child of that object.

Because the gun has been parented to the character's right hand, we now need to offset it slightly so that it lines up correctly:

1. In the **Inspector** panel, set the transform **Position** values to -5.35, -1.08, and -2 in the **X**, **Y**, and **Z** fields.

2. Set the **Rotation** values to 355, 180, and 74 in the **X**, **Y**, and **Z** fields.

3. Click the **Play** button.

4. Move the controller with the *W*, *A*, *S*, *D*, or the cursor keys.

You should see the hands and the gun move with the camera.

Saving the first-person rig as a prefab

We have a few more changes to make to our first-person rig, but before we get too far ahead it would be useful to be able to see the level that the player will interact with.

To use our first-person controller in a new scene we need to save it as a prefab:

1. In the **Project** panel, click the PACKT_Prefabs folder. Its contents should become visible in the **Assets** panel.

2. Select the FPSController parent game object in the **Hierarchy** panel and drag it into an empty space in the **Assets** panel.

This will store it as a prefab, allowing us to use it again and again.

 Dragging a game object onto another prefab in the **Assets** panel will replace the prefab, so be careful about where you drag. A dialog will pop up to warn you if you are in danger of doing this.

Adding the office-level scene

The level geometry that we will add has been saved as a prefab.

1. In the **Project** panel, locate the PACKT_Prefabs folder and click it to view its contents in the **Assets** panel.

2. In the **Assets** panel, locate LevelGeometry and drag it into the **Hierarchy** panel.

The level geometry will appear in the scene. It contains lights and colliders:

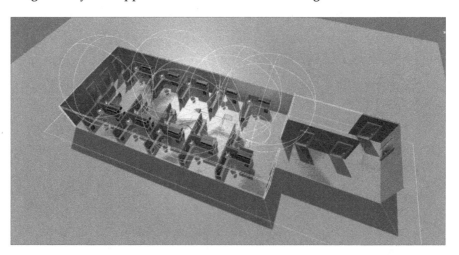

We can now delete the temporary floor object used to test the FPSController:

1. In the **Hierarchy** panel, select floorObject.

2. Press *Delete* on the keyboard (*Cmd* + *Delete* if you are working on a Mac).

3. Select and deactivate the default **Directional Light** object by selecting it in the **Hierarchy** panel and then unchecking the checkbox next to its name in the **Inspector** panel.

Next, we need to move the FPSController to a convenient position so we can see the level geometry:

1. In the **Hierarchy** panel, select the FPSController game object.

2. Use the **Move** tool to position the FPSController so that it is near the entrance to the office.

3. Switch to the **Rotate** tool and turn the FPSController so that it faces towards the space between the rows of office cubes:

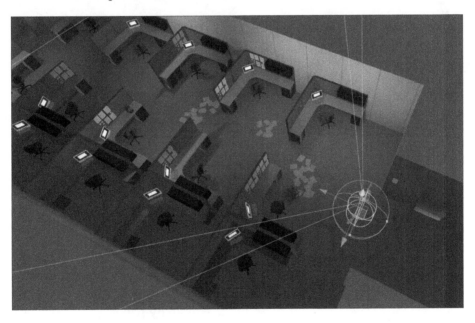

If we switch to **Play** mode at this point, we should be able to clearly see the level and move around it using the *W, A, S,* and *D* keys.

Completing the camera setup

We still need to complete our camera setup before we do anything else:

1. In the **Hierarchy** panel, select FirstPersonCharacter. If this is not visible, expand the hierarchy of its parent object FPSController by clicking the small arrow next to its name.

2. In the **Inspector** panel, change the **Field of View** to 45 degrees under the **Camera** component parameters.

Based on this setup, we can move the player_m game object forward, along the *z* axis, until we can see enough of the arms within the view.

The exact position is personal preference, but your limitations are also based on where the arm model ends:

1. Select the player_m game object in the **Hierarchy** panel.

2. Set the **Z** position to 0.25.

Now we need to save our prefab so that our changes are stored:

1. Select FPSController in the **Hierarchy** panel.

2. In the **Inspector** panel, click the **Apply** button near the top of the panel.

The prefab has been saved.

Our next task is to create an additional state for the character to allow us to shoot.

Modifying the animator controller

When we started the section, we used an existing animator controller setup with an idle animation so we could see our character's arms move.

Now we will add an additional animation sequence so we can get some action into the game:

1. In the **Hierarchy** panel, click the `player_m` game object.

2. Click the **Animator** tab in the main Unity interface.

    The animator controller named `ch3_1` should be visible in the window. Its name should be visible in the bottom right of the interface.

3. Create a new state in the animator graph by right-clicking and selecting **Create State | Empty** from the dropdown list.

4. Click the new state and rename it `Shoot` in the **Inspector** panel.

    The shoot animation has already been prepared.

5. In the **Project** panel, select the `PACKT_Animations` folder and locate `shoot`.

6. In the **Assets** panel, click the `shoot` subfolder to expand its contents.

7. Drag the `shoot` animation file into the **Shoot** state's motion field in the **Inspector** panel.

Having added the motion clip, we still need to create and set the transition.

Setting the transition

The transition will connect our two states and determine when to switch between them:

1. Right-click the **Shoot Idle** state and choose **Make Transition**.

    An arrow will appear.

2. Drag the transition line to the **Idle** state and click it to complete the transition.

Next we need to choose a parameter that the transition will operate with.

Creating a trigger parameter for the Shoot state

For this transition we will use a **Trigger** parameter, which we previously used in *Chapter 1, The Zombie Attacks!*, when we set up the zombie's attack:

1. Click the **Parameters** tab in the upper-right of the **Animator** window if it is not already active.

2. Click the **+** symbol to create a new parameter and choose **Trigger**.

3. Name this parameter Shooting.

4. Select the transition between ShootIdle and Shoot by clicking on the arrow connecting them in the **Animator** panel.

   This will bring up the transition's settings within the **Inspector** panel.

5. Select the Shooting parameter from the **Conditions** group near the bottom of the **Inspector** panel.

6. Check that the **Has Exit Time** checkbox is checked.

This will ensure that the player character will return to its **ShootIdle** state after **Shoot** has been triggered at this point, our animator controller has got two complete states, linked together with a transition:

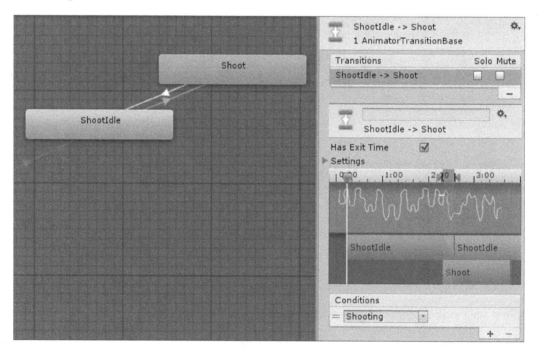

Preview the game, by pressing the **Play** button.

In the **Scene** view you should see the **Shoot** state looping constantly. In the **Animator** window this will be visualized as a blue progress bar. Pressing the **Fire1** button will not activate the **Shooting** state until we define this in a script.

Writing and implementing the character animation script

At this point, we have our basic state machine ready to go, but we still need to send a message to the animator controller to trigger the **Shoot** state.

We will do this in a short script. I am using Javascript here, but you will also find the completed code in C# in the project files:

1. In the **Project** panel, locate the `PACKT_Scripts` folder and click it to select it.

2. Create a new Javascript file in the folder by navigating to **Create | Javascript.**

3. When the file appears in the folder, click on it twice and rename it `FPSAnimation`.

4. Double-click on the file to open it in MonoDevelop.

This time we will build the code step-by-step, resulting in an animation state switch affected by the fire button.

Adding the initial code to the FPSAnimation script

The player animation script is only used in the player game object. It will connect directly with the animator controller that we just set up:

1. At the top of the script, add the following line code:

   ```
   var thisAnimator : Animator;
   ```

   The variable `thisAnimator` is defined as a type animator. This will keep track of the animator controller that this script will use.

2. Between the opening and closing brackets of the `Start` function, add the following code:

   ```
   thisAnimator = GetComponent(Animator);
   ```

   Here we define the `thisAnimator` variable as the animator component attached to the same game object as this script.

3. Add the following code to the Update function so it matches the following code:

```
function Update()
{
    if(Input.GetButton("Fire1"))
    {
        thisAnimator.SetBool("Shooting",true);
        Shoot();
    }
}
```

4. Save the script

Once it has been defined, the animator controller's parameters can be set and returned.

The if statement checks for the player input. In this case, the **Fire1** button. This is defined as the left-mouse button in the **Unity Input Manager** by default.

 Player input such as this is often checked inside of the Update function, mainly because Update runs every frame, making it highly responsive to input.

Inside the if statement, we use the variable thisAnimator, which we set up at the start of the function, setting the **Trigger** parameter Shooting (inside of the animator controller) to true. This is the operative part of the script, which will allow our shoot animation to run.

The Shoot function will then run, we will add this next:

At the bottom of the script, add the following code:

```
function Shoot()
{
    yield WaitForSeconds(0.5);
    thisAnimator.SetBool("Shooting", false);
}
```

We will leave this blank for now, but this is where we will define what happens other than the animation when the fire button is pressed.

Now that we have written our script, we need to add it to the player_m game object.

Adding the script to the player character game object

As a component, our script needs to be attached to the game object to work:

1. In the **Hierarchy** panel, select the player_m game object.

2. In the PACKT_Scripts folder, drag FPSAnimation onto player_m to add the script as a component.

   It is important that we are adding the script to the game object with the animator component attached.

3. Test the game again by clicking the **Play** button in the top center of the Unity interface.

Now when the left mouse button is pressed, the Shoot animation will play.

In this example we are checking to see whether the mouse button is being pressed, and if so, we are setting the Shooting trigger to true, which initiates the **Shoot** state in the animator controller.

Keep your **Animator** window visible (and undocked) when you press the **Play** button and you will see a blue progress bar in the **Idle** state, and then in the **Shoot** state as you press the button.

Next we will save our changes to the FPSController prefab:

1. In the **Hierarchy** panel, select the FPSController game object by clicking it once.

2. In the **Inspector** panel click the **Apply** button near the top right.

This will save the prefab and all its components and children.

This extra set of buttons in the **Inspector** panel is only available for prefab objects, it allows us to make changes and either keep or discard them.

In the next step we will allow the player to collect items.

Adding and implementing collectable objects

Typically, in a game, the player will be able to collect power-ups to increase their effectiveness, or to replace depleted life or energy.

In this game, our player will collect food to boost his health. This stage will involve adding a collectable and making the player react with a suitable animation sequence.

Instantiating the lunchBox collectable in the game level

Our first collectable is already set up as a prefab in the project files, making it easy to drag and drop into our game level without having to add components and set variables:

1. In the **Project** panel, locate the PACKT_Prefabs folder.
2. Click to expand the Pickups subfolder and locate the lunchBox prefab.
3. Drag lunchBox into the **Hierarchy** panel to instantiate it.
4. Position the prefab and navigate within the **Scene** view until it is clearly visible:

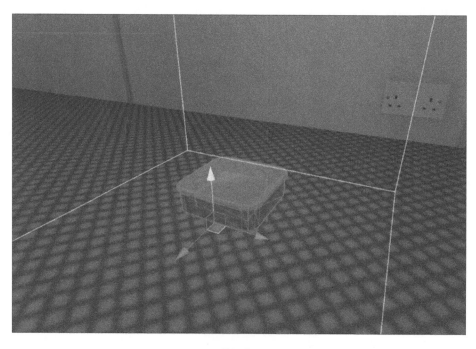

Inspecting the lunchBox collectable's components

The `lunchBox` prefab is a game object with a few components attached. We will take a look and see how it has been assembled. For doing so click the instantiated `lunchBox` in the **Hierarchy** panel to examine it a little more closely.

The prefab consists of the actual geometry, along with a point light to make it more visible within the game level. It also has a simple script which will allow us to add some functionality when it is collected.

Looking at the collectable script

We already made a start on the player animation script. The code that we need for the collectable is also quite simple. The basic script has already been set up, but we will need to add to it, to get the `lunchBox` game object to function properly in the level:

1. In the **Project** panel, click the `PACKT_Scripts` folder to view its contents in the **Assets** panel.

2. Double-click `Collectable` to open it in MonoDevelop. The script will appear as follows:

```
var sound : AudioClip;

function OnTriggerEnter (other : Collider)
{

    if (sound)
    {
    AudioSource.PlayClipAtPoint(sound, transform.position);
    }
}
```

This script is a typical definition of a power-up or a booby trap, which affects the player's status or score in some way.

It uses the `OnTriggerEnter` built-in function to set trigger code to run when the player enters its collider. The script is currently set up to play a sound effect.

Next we will add more code to ensure that the collectable game object destroys itself, preventing the player from triggering it (and receiving its benefits) again.

Implementing self destruction in the collectable script

Code placed in the Update function runs every frame, so ideally we want to set up new functions for code that is to run only once:

1. Add the following lines of code to the bottom of the script:

```
function Remove()
    {
        Destroy(gameObject);
    }
```

Remove is a new custom function. It removes the instanced prefab from the game. It happens instantly, so any particle or sound effects should be added to the preceding function.

We still need to run this function at the end of OnTriggerEnter.

2. Before the last curly bracket in the OnTriggerEnter function, add the following line:

```
Remove();
```

3. Save the script and add it to the lunchBox prefab by dragging it onto the instance in the **Hierarchy** panel or the **Inspector** panel.

4. Test the script by positioning the instantiated lunchBox a few meters from the player character game object.

5. Click the **Game** view tab in the top center of the Unity interface and deselect the **Maximize on Play** button by clicking it.

6. Press the **Play** button.

7. Move the player character towards the `lunchBox` collectable.

    The lunchbox will disappear (from the **Scene** view and the **Hierarchy** panel) when contact is made:

In the next section we will be setting up the player character's response when the `lunchBox` is collected.

Setting up the player character's response

We will start by adding an additional state to the player character's animator controller.

Unlike with the shoot animation, the pickup animation will only run when the character is in collision with the `lunchBox`. We will need to stop other animations playing to enable the pickup animation to play through.

In order to view this animation, we will create an additional camera and set it up to become active for the duration of the animation sequence. Lastly, we will implement a very simple player status script so that we can see the character's health value increase when he collects the `lunchBox`.

Adding the Pickup state to the animator controller

As we are adding a new animation sequence, we need to add a new state to contain this:

1. In the **Hierarchy** panel, click to select player_m.

2. Click the **Animator** tab in the top center of the Unity interface to view the selected object's animator controller.

3. Right-click somewhere in the empty space to create a new state by navigating to **Create State | Empty**.

4. In the **Inspector** panel, rename this state Pickup.

5. In the **Project** panel, click the PACKT_Animations folder to expose its contents in the **Assets** panel.

6. Locate the pickup subfolder and click it to view its contents.

7. Drag the pickup animation (identified by the gray play button icon) into the **Pickup** state's **motion** field in the **Inspector** panel.

Having specified the animation sequence used in the state, we need to set the transitions and parameter that will activate this state.

Setting the Pickup state's transitions and parameter

Importantly, the new **Pickup** state will only be connected by transitions to the **ShootIdle** state, otherwise we risk overriding the player's attack.

Imagine that the player character is backing away from a horde of zombies rushing towards him, when he stumbles over lunchBox and has to stop shooting to pick it up!

Prioritizing player states is an important factor when considering game play. Mecanim makes this really easy because it shows us exactly how the character's states connect.

Transitioning between the ShootIdle and Pickup states

States can have multiple transitions connecting them to other states. For the moment, our **Pickup** state only needs to be connected to the **ShootIdle** state:

1. In the **Animator** window, right-click the **ShootIdle** state and choose **Make Transition**.

2. Drag the transition line to the **Pickup** state and click on it to complete the transition.

3. Create the return transition in the same way from the **Pickup** state to the **ShootIdle** state.

The new transitions are connecting the states, but currently have default settings. Next we need to add an appropriate parameter.

Creating and adding the parameter

Like variables in a script, parameters created in the animator controller can be used multiple times. Here we will create another **Trigger** parameter that will switch the **Pickup** state on:

1. In the **Parameters** box, click the **+** symbol to create a new parameter.
2. Choose **Trigger**.
3. Name the new parameter `Picking` and leave its radio button deactivated.
4. Click the **Idle** to **Pickup** transition.
5. In the **Inspector** panel, scroll down until you see the **Conditions** box.
6. Set the condition to `Picking`, and make sure that the Boolean marker is set to **True**.

This will ensure that the **Pickup** state is only activated when the `Picking` is triggered:

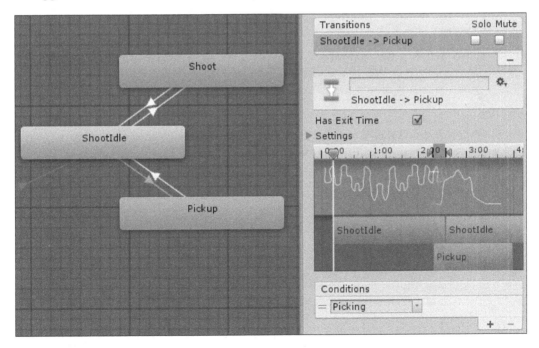

The next step will involve creating the new camera that we will use during the pickup animation.

Creating the pickup camera

We will add a new camera to view the player character's pickup animation sequence more clearly. Briefly switching cameras will make it unnecessary for us to alter the main camera script, which is used throughout the majority of the game level. It will also make it obvious to the player that the character is picking up an item:

1. Create a `Camera` game object by navigating to **Game Object | Create Other | Camera**.

2. In the **Inspector** panel, rename the game object `pickupCamera`.

3. Delete all of the game object's components except **Camera**.

   When we setup the first-person camera, we reduced the near clipping planes so that the player geometry would not be clipped out. We need to do the same thing for the `pickupCamera`.

4. In the **Camera** component's settings in the **Inspector** panel, set the **Near** clipping plane value to `0.05`.

   As we want this camera to render on top of the first-person camera we need to give it a higher priority.

5. Further down in the **Inspector** panel, set the **Camera** component's **Depth** value to `1`.

   This makes it unnecessary to deactivate the first-person camera when we temporarily switch to the pickup camera. This also means that we do not need an additional audio listener component to hear any sounds which are played.

6. In the **Project** panel, locate the `PACKT_Scripts` folder and click it, to view its contents in the **Assets** panel.

7. Drag the `pickupCamera` script onto the `pickupCamera` game object that we just created.

There are a few more steps to take to complete the pickup camera.

Finalizing the pickup camera prefab

We will be changing the position and rotation of the camera in our script, but we need a default target that the camera can point at:

1. Create a sphere game object in the scene by navigating to **Game Object | 3D Object | Sphere**.

2. In the **Inspector** panel rename it `defaultTarget`.

3. Set the game object's scale **X**, **Y**, and **Z** values to `0.1`.

4. Delete the **Sphere Collider** component by right-clicking on the settings icon in the top-right corner of the component's parameter list and choosing **Remove Component**.

   We will keep the **Mesh Renderer** component for now so we can make sure the target is lined up correctly.

   We need to group the `pickupCamera` and `defaultTarget` together so they can be instantiated in the game.

5. Create a new empty game object by navigating to **Game Object |
   Create Empty**.

6. Rename the empty object `camParent`.

7. In the **Hierarchy** panel, drag `pickupCamera` and then `defaultTarget` onto `camParent` to make them children of this game object.

8. Select each of the game objects and zero out their position and rotation values in the **Inspector** panel.

9. Select `defaultTarget` and set its **Position Z** value to `2`.

10. Check that it is positioned directly in front of the camera by selecting the camera in the **Hierarchy** panel.

    The camera's view will be displayed as an inset in the corner of the main **Scene** view.

    The `defaultTarget` should appear as a small sphere in the center of the view.

11. When you have verified where it should be, select it in the **Hierarchy** and deactivate its mesh renderer by checking the box next to the **Mesh Renderer** component.

    Finally, we will save the whole hierarchy as a prefab, allowing it to be instantiated in the game when we need it.

12. In the **Project** panel, click to select the `PACKT_Prefabs` folder.

13. Select the `camParent` game object in the **Hierarchy** panel and drag it into an empty area of the **Assets** panel.

    The game object name will turn blue in the **Hierarchy** panel, indicating that it is now an instance of a prefab. Delete the instance from the scene by selecting it and hitting *Delete* (or *Cmd + Delete* on a Mac).

Next we will create a simple player status script to enable the player to get something from the pickup.

Looking at the player status script

The player status script keeps track of the player's current condition in the game. This often includes health and other numerical values that change during gameplay:

1. In the **Project** panel, click to expand the PACKT_Scripts folder in the **Assets** panel.

2. Locate PlayerStatus and double-click to open it in MonoDevelop.

This is what we currently have in the PlayerStatus script:

```
var health : int = 10;
var healthLimit : int = 10;

function AddHealth (increase : int)
{
    health += increase;

    if (health > healthLimit)
{
        health = healthLimit;
    }

}


function AddDamage (damage : int)
{
    health-=damage;

    if (health <= 0)
    {
        Die();
    }
}
function Die()
{
    Debug.Log("You Died");
}
```

The first variable, health sets the starting health value as an integer or whole number. Next, healthMax sets the maximum value that health can reach.

The custom function AddHealth increases the health value by an amount specified by the value increase which will be sent to the script.

The `if` statement contained within the function will capture health with the `maxHealth` value so that it does not exceed this number even if the player picks up lots of lunchBoxes when we do not need them.

The custom function `AddDamage` works in the same way, but decrements health rather than increasing it using an integer value called `damage`. When health reaches zero we run the custom function `Die`.

No fancy effects at this point, just a message appearing in the console informing the player that he or she is dead. We can test this later on, but for now we will get back to the pickup interaction.

Adding the PlayerStatus script to the player character game object

The `PlayerStatus` script is added directly to the player character, so that it can be accessed and affected by other scripts:

1. In the **Hierarchy** panel, select the `player_m` game object.

2. Drag `PlayerStatus` onto `player_m` to add it as a component.

The player is now capable of losing and gaining health.

Next, we will make the necessary changes to the `Collectable` and `FPSAnimation` scripts.

Updating the Collectable script

We need to add some extra functions to our scripts in order to facilitate the picking up:

1. Open the `Collectable` script in MonoDevelop.

2. At the top of the script, add the following variables:

   ```
   var increase : int;
   var playerObj : GameObject;
   var pickingCamera : GameObject;
   var playerCamera : Transform;
   var headBone : Transform;
   var triggered : boolean = false;
   ```

   The value increase is the amount of health that the collectable will give the player when he picks it up. We are setting this to 1 by default

   The variable `playerObj` will store the player game object. We could also locate the player with its tag if we wanted to.

Next, `pickingCamera` will store the prefab containing the camera which we need to instantiate when the player picks the item up.

We also store a reference to the first-person camera with `playerCamera`, so we can access its transform data.

The Boolean variable `triggered` will be used to check whether the collectable is currently being picked up, so that it does not trigger multiple times.

Lastly, `headBone` will store the transform of the bone in the character's hierarchy that we will parent the pickup camera to.

3. Add the following code to the top of the `OnTriggerEnter` before the `if (sound)` statement that we already added:

```
if(triggered == false)
{
    triggered = true;
    var playerState = playerObj.GetComponent(PlayerStatus);
    var playerAnim = playerObj.GetComponent(FPSAnimation);

    playerState.AddHealth(increase);
    playerAnim.Pick();

    RunCam();
```

At the bottom of the function delete the `Remove();` line and add another closing curly bracket to complete our `if(triggered)` statement.

Here we check to make sure that the collectable is not already being triggered. If `triggered` is not true, we run the contained code by setting `triggered` to `true`.

We add two new local variables to access the `PlayerStatus` and `FPSAnimation` scripts and then run functions in each of these to add to the `health` value and run an animation respectively. Lastly we run the `RunCam` function. This will contain the code that operates the pickup camera.

4. Add the following code to the bottom of the script:

```
function RunCam()
{
    var pickTrans = transform;
    var addCamObj : GameObject = Instantiate(pickingCamera,
    headBone.position, playerCamera.rotation);
    addCamObj.transform.parent = headBone;
```

```
addCamObj.transform.GetChild(0).SendMessage
("SentTarget", pickTrans);
yield WaitForSeconds(0.5);
Remove();
}
```

We start by creating two local variables. The first, `pickTrans` is set as the transform that this script is attached to.

Secondly, `addCamObj` is defined as type `gameObject`, this will store the instantiated object so we can further modify its position and rotation. In the next line we instantiate the prefab, setting its position to match `headBone` and its rotation to match the existing player camera.

We make `addCamObj` the child of `headBone`. As a bone in the `player_m` hierarchy, `headBone` already animates when the pickup animation plays.

In the next line we locate the first child object within `AddCamObj`, which is the `pickupCamera`. This is sent the message `"SentTarget"`, with the variable `pickTrans` which we just defined. This effectively sends the collectable's transform as the camera's target.

We add a short pause with the yield `WaitForSeconds` method, before running the `Remove` function which destroys the collectable game object, and which already exists at the bottom of our script.

5. Save the script.

The pause is handled differently in C#. Take a look at the final commented code in the project files for details.

Our next step will involve hooking up variables, before we move on to updating the other scripts.

Hooking up variables in the collectable script

The script now accesses plenty of other game objects. We need to connect these in the main unity interface:

1. In the **Hierarchy** panel, *Alt* + click the small arrow next to the `FPSController` game object to fully expand its hierarchy.

2. Select `lunchBox`.

   Its components will become visible in the **Inspector** panel.

3. Drag `player_m` from the **Hierarchy** panel into the **Player Obj** slot under the **Collectable (Script)** component in the **Inspector** panel.

4. Drag the `FirstPersonCharacter` game object onto the **Player Camera** slot.

5. Scroll down in the **Hierarchy** panel until you find `zombie_m_Head`.

6. Drag this onto the `headBone` slot in the **Inspector** panel.

7. In the **Project** panel, click the `PACKT_Prefabs` folder to view its contents in the **Assets** panel.

8. Locate `camParent` and drag this onto the **Picking Camera** slot in the **Inspector** panel.

In the next section, we will make some changes to the `FPSAnimation` script.

Updating the FPSAnimation script

We created the `FPSAnimation` script and attached it to the `player_m` game object earlier in this chapter.

Currently it is used to set the trigger, transitioning to the **Shoot** state in the player's animator controller. Here we will update it to trigger the **Pickup** state:

1. Locate the `FPSAnimation` script in the `PACKT_Animations` folder.

2. Double-click on it, to open it in MonoDevelop.

3. At the bottom of the script, add the following functions:

```
function Pick()
{
    thisAnimator.SetTrigger("Picking");
}
```

The `Pick` function accesses animator controller and uses the same `SetTrigger` function to set the Mecanim trigger `Picking`.

Unlike `Fire`, `Pick` does not use input but is run from another script—the `Collectable` script that we just updated.

4. Save the script.

The last script we need to update is `pickup`, the script attached to `pickupCamera`.

Modifying the pickup script

The bare bones `pickup` script was already included in the project files. It was attached to `pickupCamera` when we setup the `camParent` prefab earlier in this chapter.

We can start by taking a look at the current code:

1. In the **Project** panel, click the PACKT_Scripts folder to view its contents in the **Assets** panel.

2. Locate the pickup script and double-click it to open it in MonoDevelop:

```
var life : float = 1.5;

function SentTarget(pickTrans : Transform)
{
    transform.LookAt(pickTrans);
    yield WaitForSeconds(life);
    ReturnTarget();
}

function ReturnTarget()
{
    Destroy(transform.parent.gameObject);
}
```

The script contains single variable, life, which defines the duration that the prefab is created before it is destroyed. During this time the pickup camera is active.

The custom function SentTarget is run from the Collectable script when the player enters its trigger. It is sent the collectable object's transform to use as a target. This is currently set up using the transform.LookAt method.

When the life duration is up, the ReturnTarget function runs, destroying the parent game object — the object which pickupCamera is a child of.

If we test the game at this point, the camera switch will work, but the transition is a little jarring. We need to smooth the transition between the first-person camera and the pickup camera.

We will start by adding some more variables. Near the top of the script add the following code just below the existing variable:

```
var origTarget : Transform;
var pickTarget : Transform;
var damping : float = 5.0;
var camOffset : Vector3;
```

The variable origTarget will be used to store the pickupCamera object's original rotation so we can transition back to it.

The next variable, `pickTarget` will store the new target sent to the script from the collectable.

Lastly, `damping` is used to delay the transition so the camera does not snap back quite so quickly.

3. Now replace the code inside of the `SentTarget` function with the following code:

```
pickTarget = pickTrans;
var lookAtPosition : Vector3 = pickTarget.position;
    lookAtPosition.y = transform.position.y;
    lookAtPosition.z = transform.position.z;
    var rotation = Quaternion.LookRotation(lookAtPosition -
    transform.position);
    transform.rotation =
    Quaternion.Slerp(transform.rotation, rotation,
    Time.deltaTime * damping);
    yield WaitForSeconds(life);
    ReturnTarget();
```

We define `pickTarget` as equal to `pickTrans`, the `transform` variable is sent from collectable.

Next we replace the `transform.LookAt` method with some more specialized code that will allow us to transition between the camera targets smoothly. This starts with the definition of a new local `Vector3` variable, `lookAtPosition`.

In the next two lines we override the sent transform's **Y** and **Z** values with the `pickCamera` object's existing transform data, so we end up only using the **X** value. This will allow the camera to dip rather than twisting towards the target.

Next we define another local variable, `rotation` using the `Quaternion.LookRotation` method. This allows us to measure the difference in rotation between the current target position and new target position.

The next line of code causes the camera to rotate from the current rotation to the new rotation value over time and with damping.

Next we put in our pause using the `yield WaitForSeconds` method and using our `life` float variable. This value needs to be sufficiently long to allow the pickup animation to play.

Finally we run our `ReturnTarget` function to get the camera back to where it was.

4. Add the following code to the `Return Target` function before the existing line of code:

```
var origPosition : Vector3 = origTarget.position;
    origPosition.y = transform.position.y;
    origPosition.z = transform.position.z;
    var rotation = Quaternion.LookRotation(origPosition -
    transform.position);
    transform.rotation =
    Quaternion.Slerp(transform.rotation, rotation,
    Time.deltaTime * damping);
```

Here we reverse the procedure, transitioning in the same way from the current rotation to a new rotation defined in the variable `origTarget`.

5. Now, save the script.

Lastly, we need to hook up a single variable and adjust the transform values of the `pickCamera` object:

1. Minimize MonoDevelop.
2. In the **Project** panel, click the `PACKT_Prefabs` folder to view its contents in the **Assets** panel.
3. Locate the `camParent` prefab and click the small arrow to expand its hierarchy within the **Assets** panel.
4. Click the `pickupCamera` child object which appears beside it.

   The `Pickup (Script)` components variables will become visible in the **Inspector** panel.

   We need to leave the `Pick Target` variable slot empty as this is sent from `collectable` at runtime.
5. Drag the `defaultTarget` child game object from the **Assets** panel onto the **Orig Target** slot to define it.
6. In the `pickupCamera` object's **Transform Position** fields at the top of the Inspector, enter -0.25 in the **Y** field and 0.25 in the **Z** field.

These values will move the camera slightly closer to the collectable, minimizing the chance of seeing the ends of the player arms. If you adjusted the `player_m` position differently you may want to experiment with the values.

Changes made directly to prefabs like this will be effected instantly. We can now test the `lunchBox` collectable.

Testing the lunchBox collectable

We will test the effects of the collectable and the pickup animation by adding a few more instances of the lunchBox game objects to our level:

1. In the **Hierarchy** panel, select the lunchBox game object.

2. Hit *Ctrl + D* three times to duplicate the game object (use *Cmd + D* if you are working on a Mac).

3. Use the **Move** tool to reposition the new instances of the lunchBox so they are spaced out within the environment.

4. Click to select the player_m game object

5. In the **Inspector** panel, scroll down until you can clearly see the health variable in the **Player Status** component.

6. Set the health value to 7.

7. Click the **Game** view tab.

8. If it is active, click to deactivate the **Maximize on Play** button near the top of the interface.

9. Press the **Play** button to preview the game.

10. Navigate the player towards the lunchBox collectables.

We will get something like this:

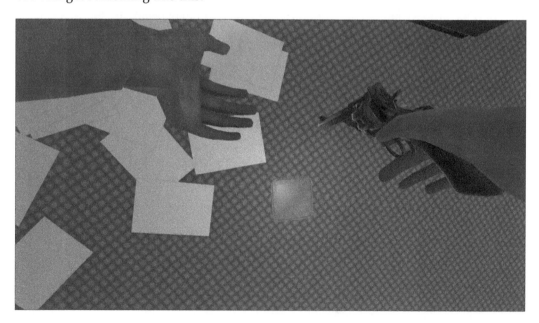

When the player collides with each of the collectables, the `Pickup` animation will play and the collectable will disappear.

The `health` value in the **Inspector** panel will increase up to the maximum amount.

The last `lunchBox` collectible will still disappear, but the `health` value will not exceed the number defined in the `healthLimit`.

Summary

In this chapter, we explored various aspects of environmental interaction. We started by setting up a first-person controller to work with our player character model. We then created a state machine in the **Animator** window for our player and added the appropriate motion clips. We set up the switch between states using a player animation script.

Finally, we added health power-ups for the player to collect in the level, and scripted a player response with the use of an additional camera and the player status script.

In the next chapter, we will return to our enemy characters and demonstrate how motion capture data can be implemented within a Mecanim-ready character.

We will define frame ranges in a source file to create useable loops, which can then be set up in the zombie character's state machine.

4
Working with
Motion Capture Data

As a method of translating real-world movement into a usable digital file, motion capture crosses a major boundary in computer graphics. In more complex animation sequences, traditional keyframe animation techniques are sometimes too time consuming. With motion capture processes becoming more affordable and available, many independent game developers are exploiting this technology to add a dynamic edge to their projects.

In this chapter we will:

- Explain the characteristics of motion capture files
- Demonstrate the creation of two distinct walk cycles from one motion capture file
- Set up a simple scene, animator controller, and script to test the resulting motion clips

This chapter will feature the male zombie character that was imported and prepared in *Chapter 1, The Zombie Attacks!*. If you worked through this chapter, you can proceed with the same file, or use the readied model provided in the project files.

Introduction to motion capture sequences and their characteristics

In short, motion capture is an attempt to record the simultaneous movement of items (usually the joints or bones of the human body).

Motion capture sequences have been successfully created in a number of ways:

- Motion capture suits contain a number of sensors that return the actual joint rotations as an actor is performing an action
- Optical motion capture often uses cameras to pinpoint the position of key markers within three-dimensional space.

In the past, both of these methods required special equipment and, consequently, were very expensive. Advances in movement control in game consoles such as Wii, Playstation, and Xbox have made simple motion capture using markerless motion capture more affordable and accessible.

The motion capture sequences provided as examples with this book were captured with a Kinect sensor connected to a PC. Motion capture is used in video games for the same reasons that it is used in visual effects in the movie industry.

The convincing movement of the human form is sufficiently complex to take a long time to perfect using traditional keyframe animation. Rather than just animate a series of joints or bones, you have to consider how these joints and bones move together. Secondary animation effects, such as balance and counterweight, are vitally important for the human motion to look real. In fast or particularly energetic sequences, these can be very difficult to achieve.

Like traditional animation, motion capture is done with a target frame rate in order to optimize quality and keep the resulting file sizes within useable boundaries. Using the economical methods available, the number of bones or joints that can be captured is limited, and there is very little support for the capture of facial expression and complex hand animation. Neither of these are substantially supported in the current version of Unity anyway.

Because of the amount of data captured, it is a good idea to limit the length of each motion capture take. Trimming and cleaning up motion capture sequences is also an important step in using this technology efficiently within the parameters of game development.

Using a motion capture sequence with a pre-rigged model

To demonstrate the use of motion capture data in Mecanim we will continue with the male zombie character that we worked with in *Chapter 1, The Zombie Attacks!*.

Getting started

We will begin this demonstration with the basic scene we assembled in the first chapter.

1. Open the scene by navidating to **File | Open Scene**.

2. In the scene file dialog that opens up, select Chapter4_Start from the PACKT_Scenes folder.

    The scene contains our zombie_m character and a ground plane, and is lit with the default directional light and skybox.

    The character already has an animator controller attached to it, though it only has the idle and attack animation sequences that we added in *Chapter 1, The Zombie Attacks!*.

3. Move the default camera to a position where it clearly shows the zombie_m character and the extent of the groundPlane in front of it:

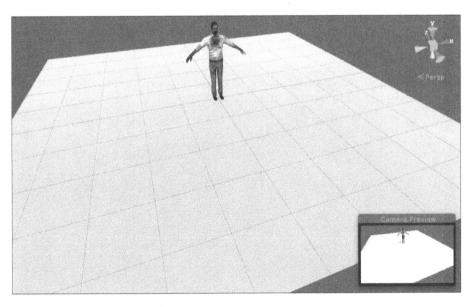

Setting up the scene in this way will make it easier to clearly see our motion sequences.

Importing the motion capture sequence

The motion capture sequence contains the animated bones or markers that are stored in the file when the motion is captured. Mecanim allows us to transfer this data to our character's rig, which will usually have a different hierarchy of bones or joints than the source FBX.

When we import the motion capture file, Unity will set up the asset with an Avatar, which will make it compatible with our existing character:

1. In the unzipped project files that you downloaded for this book, locate the folder named motionCapture.

2. Open the folder to locate zombie_walk.FBX.

   This file contains the motion capture sequence that we will be using in this chapter.

3. Back in Unity, locate the PACKT_Animations folder in the **Project** panel.

4. Click it once to display its contents in the **Assets** panel.

5. Drag zombie_walk.FBX into the **Assets** panel.

6. Now that it has been imported, click zombie_walk to select it.

Next, we will need to make some changes to the import settings.

Adjusting the import settings

The **Inspector** panel will display the FBX file's import settings, allowing us to adjust them.

Under the **Model** tab, make sure that the scale is consistent with your model. In this case, the scale should be set to 1 by default.

We are only importing the animation here, so many of the checkboxes that deal with the mesh can be ignored:

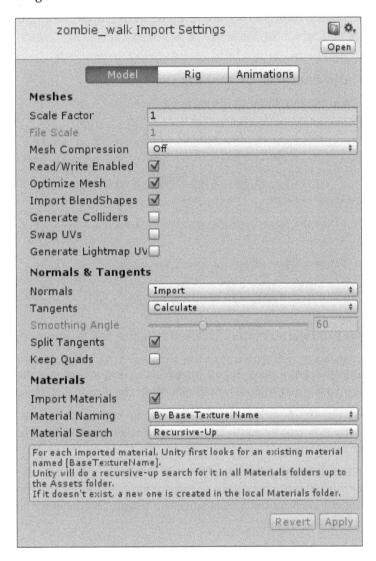

Adjusting the rig import settings

As we demonstrated earlier, the **Model** import settings are where we specify the scale and format of the data that we are bringing in to Unity. We still need to adjust the **Rig** settings to define how the skeleton is processed into an Avatar that Mecanim can use:

1. In the **Inspector** panel, click the **Rig** tab.

2. Set the **Animation Type** to **Humanoid**.

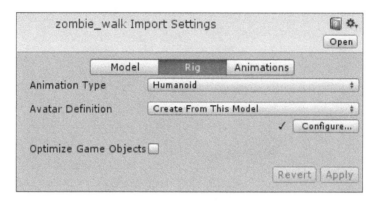

3. Click the **Configure...** button. This will initialize the Avatar mapping diagram.

    Often, Mecanim will do most of the work for you, but it is always a good idea to double check the mapping of the bones to make sure that the right bones have been assigned to the right slots within the character's Avatar.

    If you are using models and animations from different sources (as is the case here), this will be a crucial step, as the skeletons will not have the same naming conventions.

    Sometimes there are additional bones in the arms, spine, and legs and we need to make sure that the bones we assign are in the same position in both rigs. If there are any compatibility issues, we can usually fix these within Mecanim.

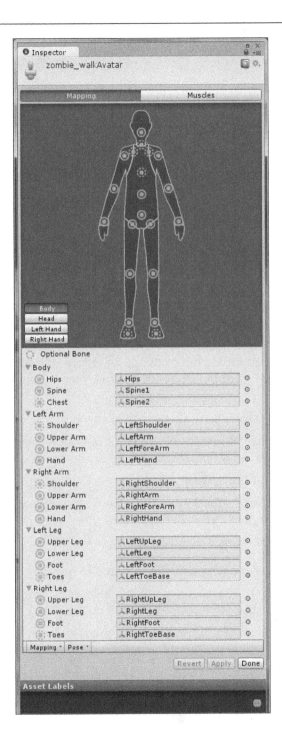

Any errors in the mapping will be displayed with red warning labels in the viewport.

4. Once you are happy with the mapping, click **Done** to save the changes to the Avatar.

Next we will define the range of the sequence in the **Animations** import tab.

Adjusting the sequence in the Animations tab

The **Animations** import settings are where we specify the range of the animation and whether it is a loop or a single-shot sequence:

1. Click the **Animations** tab in the **Inspector** panel.

2. Make sure that the **Import Animation** checkbox is checked. This should be the case by default.

3. Click the **Story anim stack** clip in the **Clips** list to access the additional animation settings.

   When we imported the animation sequences in the last chapter, they were already prepared for us, but in this case we have a long animation sequence that needs to be trimmed to create a proper looping walk sequence for our zombie.

   By default, all frames of the sequence are used in the current animation clip.

   The **Animation Preview** panel at the bottom of the **Inspector** panel currently shows a default humanoid character. Let's preview the animation sequence on the zombie_m character instead.

4. Drag the zombie_m game object from the **Hierarchy** panel onto the **Animation Preview** panel.

   The display should update to show the male zombie.

5. In the **Preview** panel, click the **Play** button to preview the sequence.

6. The animation sequence shows the zombie's walk. Importantly, in this motion capture file, there are several full cycles.

   The walk sequence is not completely regular, and there are variations consistent with what we would expect for a zombie's walk.

7. Rename the sequence zwalk01 by typing this into the name field just below the **Clips** list.

8. Hit **Enter** to store the name change.

   Next we will specify the start and end frames of the sequence.

9. Click the **Clamp Range** button, to allow you to specify the start and end of the new cycle within the source sequence.

10. Preview the animation and find the point in the walk sequence where the left foot comes to its full forward extent for the first time.

11. Drag the **Start** frame tag to this point or type the number of the frame into the **Start** field.

    Frame 180 should be about right, but if you have chosen a different frame, this is also okay.

12. Drag the **End** frame tag to the point in the sequence where the first cycle ends.

    This will be where the left foot comes to its full forward extent for the second time.

    Frame 225 should be about right. This number could also be typed into the **End** field.

When you choose the end frame of a cycle, keep an eye on the colored circles on the right of the **Inspector** panel. These help you to locate an appropriate start and end of a loop. All circles will turn green if you have a perfect match.

These circles represent the **Local Bone Rotations**, **Root Transform Rotation**, **Root Transform Position (Y)**, and **Root Transform Position (XZ)**.

It is okay if not all of these are displayed in green. At the moment, the first of these is the one that you should be the most concerned about. A green circle is the best match; yellow is the next best.

13. Check the **Loop Time** and **Loop Pose** checkboxes to make sure that the sequence is interpreted as a cycle.

Animation sequences always loop in the preview panel, but you will need to specify that they are loops in the **Animations** import settings for them to actually loop when they run in the game.

14. In the **Root Transform Position (Y)** group, set the **Based Upon (at Start)** value to Feet using the drop-down list.

15. Check the **Bake into Pose** checkbox for this group to make sure that the position of the feet in the pose are identified.

    This will help to make sure that the feet do not penetrate the ground plane as the character walks.

16. Leave the remaining parameters with their default values.

17. Click the **Apply** button to store the changes.

18. Preview the animation again, it should now start with the frame that you selected:

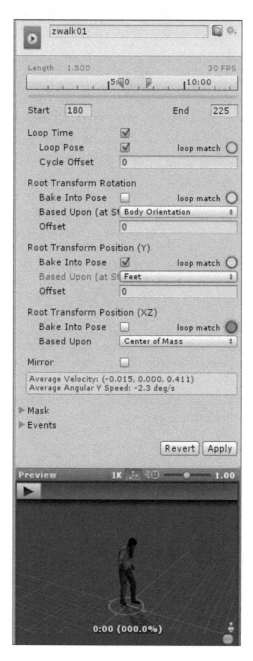

Creating the second walk cycle

We will get a little more mileage out of this motion capture sequence by creating another walk cycle that uses a different portion of the original animation clip.

As our game will involve multiple zombies walking around in our scene at any given time, this will help to add some variety. We could even set up these animation clips to play randomly:

1. Click on the **+** symbol in the **Clips** list to add another animation clip. The start and end tags will be reset to their original positions at the beginning and end of the original animation clip.

2. Rename the new clip `zwalk02`.

3. Again click the **Clamp Range** button.

4. Making sure that the new clip is selected, move the **Start** frame tag to the second instance in which the left foot has reached its forward extent, around frame 225.

   This is the same frame as the end frame of the first walk cycle.

5. Move the **End** frame tag to the next instance in which the left foot has reached its extent. Frame 264 should be a good end frame.

6. Make sure to check **Loop Time** and **Loop Pose**, and check the colored circles for a good match.

7. As before, select **Feet** as the value in the **Based Upon (at Start)** drop-down list in the **Root Transform Position (Y)** group, and check the **Bake into Pose** checkbox.

8. Click the **Apply** button to save the changes made to `zwalk02`.

9. Preview the animation.

Despite being derived from the same motion capture sequence, the two sequences should appear distinctly different.

In order to play the animations in the scene, we will need to add them to the animator controller and reference them in a short script to determine when each will play.

Adding the new motion clips to the animation controller

In the game, we would probably want a single zombie to use only one walk sequence, but for testing purposes we will set up a script to switch between the two prepared cycles.

We will have our zombie walk automatically when we start the game, and have him switch animations when the *B* key is pressed:

1. In the **Project** panel, navigate to the PACKT_Controllers folder.

2. Drag walkTest onto the **Controller** slot in the zombie's animator component in the **Inspector** panel.

3. Activate the **Animator** tab, next to **Scene** and **Game** views in the center panel, by clicking it.

> If the **Animator** tab is not visible, it can be activated from the **Menu** tab by navigating to **Windows** | **Animator**.

If you expand or *Alt* + drag the **Animator** window, you will see that it contains only two additional states: **Walk01** and **Walk02**:

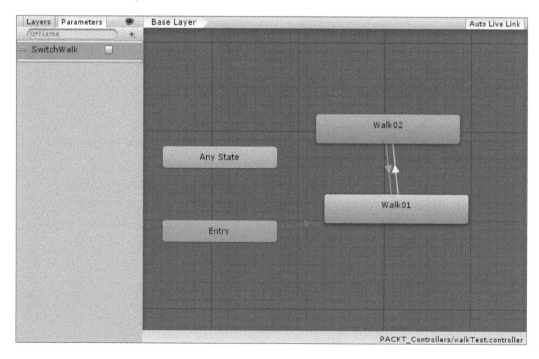

The transitions between these two states are set up with a boolean parameter called `SwitchWalk`, which is set to `false` (off) by default, shown in the **Parameters** box with an unchecked checkbox.

4. Click the **Walk01** state and drag the `zwalk01` animation clip into the first motion field.

5. Do the same for **Walk02**, assigning `zwalk02` to the second motion field.

The next step will involve triggering the transition between the states in a short script.

Creating a script to see both animation loops in action

In order to see the difference between our two walk animation loops, we will set up a simple script to enable them to play in turn:

1. In the **Project** panel, select the PACKT_Scripts folder and create a new Javascript file within it by navigating to **Create | Javascript**.

2. Name the script `zombieWalkTest01`.

3. Double-click on the file to open it in MonoDevelop.

4. Replace the default code in the script with the following code:

```
var zombieControl : Animator;
var walkBool : boolean = false;

function Start ()
{
    zombieControl = GetComponent(Animator);
}

function Update ()
{
    if(Input.GetKeyDown("b"))
    {
        walkBool = !walkBool;
        zombieControl.SetBool("SwitchWalk", walkBool);
    }
}
```

At the top of the script, we create the variable `zombieControl` to maintain a connection between the character game object's animator component.

We create a boolean named `walkBool` that will be used within this script to determine when to switch between our two animation states. This is set to `false` by default.

Within the `Start` function, we define the first variable as the animator component attached to the same game object as the script using the `GetComponent` method. We also set the Mecanim boolean `SwitchWalk` to `walkBool`, which has already been set to `false` as its default state.

In the `Update` function, we check for down input from the *B* key. When this condition is met, we switch the `walkBool` boolean. We also set the Mecanim boolean `SwitchWalk` to the value returned by `walkBool`.

This is a very simple example of how to set up a two-state behavior controlled with user input. The script could easily be adapted to respond to environmental triggers.

We will go into more detail with this in *Chapter 9, Controlling Enemy Animation with AI and Triggers*, which deals with enemy behavior.

Adding the script and previewing the animation switch

We have set up the zombie's animator controller but we still need to attach the script before we can test the animation loops:

1. Select the `zombie_m` game object in the **Hierarchy** panel to expose its properties in the **Inspector** panel.
2. Add the script by dragging it onto the game object in the **Hierarchy** panel. `zombieWalkTest01` will show up as a script component in the **Inspector** panel.
3. Press **Play** to preview the animation.
4. Once the zombie has cycled through his first animation a couple of times, press *B* on the keyboard and see the second walk cycle run.

This will continue until you hit the *B* key again:

There should be some noticeable differences between the two walk cycles. Small variations in the pose and movement of the joints will give each walk cycle its own distinct character.

Summary

In this chapter, we introduced the key characteristics of motion capture data and showed the advantages of using it in a project. We introduced the **Animation** import settings, demonstrated how seamless loops can be created, and how a number of unique walk cycles could be derived from a single motion capture sequence.

In the next chapter, we will look at animation retargeting and how an animation clip can be used for characters of different types. We will look at how optional bones come into play and how variations in characters can be accommodated within Mecanim's toolset.

5
Retargeting Animation

In *Chapter 4*, *Working with Motion Capture Data*, we used Mecanim to create two unique walk cycles from an imported motion capture file. This chapter will demonstrate how motion sequences such as these can be reused for different characters.

Mecanim's robust animation toolset allows users to reuse animation sequences in different characters. Provided that both characters use the **Humanoid** animation type (specified in the **Import** settings), a great deal of variation within skeletons is possible. Mecanim will identify and convert animation sequences based on the bone's position in the skeletal hierarchy, eliminating the necessity of identical (and identically named) rigs.

If you are creating animation sequences from scratch using traditional keyframe animation techniques, it does not take much extra time to animate extra bones, such as ponytails and accessories in a character's rig. However, when it becomes necessary to use pre-made animations and incorporate motion capture data, it can be a time-consuming process to adapt and refine a generic animation to fit a key character within the game.

In this chapter, we will demonstrate Mecanim's animation retargeting capacity with the following objectives:

- Copying and modifying an animation sequence for a different character
- Adjusting animation import settings to get a better fit
- Modifying muscle parameters to limit a character's range of movement
- Using animation masks and layers and accommodating these in the script
- Varying a walk sequence using animation masks
- Retargeting the male walk animation for the female zombie character

To demonstrate the retargeting capabilities of Mecanim, we will continue with the walk sequences created for the male zombie in the previous chapter, this time adapting one of the walk cycles for his female counterpart.

Loading the scene

This time, the starting scene has been prepared. It includes a basic environment, lighting and the zombie_f prefab already set up to work with Mecanim.

In the Unity project, open the scene Chapter5_Start. The scene will load. The female zombie already has an Avatar, and has an animator component attached to it, containing a single, idling animation unique to the character.

The zombie_f prefab also has a short script, which is set up ready to play the idle and walk sequences:

Adding and previewing the animation

At this point we will add one of the walk sequences to the zombie's animator controller:

1. Click the **Animator** tab to view the character's animator controller.

2. In the **Animator** window, click the **Walk** state to view its parameters in the **Inspector** panel.

3. In the **Project** panel, click the PACKT_Animations folder to view its contents in the **Assets** panel.

4. Locate the zombie_walk asset and click the small arrow to the right of its icon to view its contents.

5. Drag zWalk01 from the **Assets** panel into the **Walk** state's **Motion** field in the **Inspector** panel to add it to the state machine.

6. Press the **Play** button in the top-center of the Unity interface to preview the game:

The female zombie character will idle for a short time before launching into the walk sequence. It should be obvious that there are a few issues with the walk sequence:

- When the character starts walking, she floats to a position above the ground
- During the walk cycle, the character's arms intersect with her torso
- The ponytail does not move along with the rest of the character:

These issues will be fixed in the animation import settings.

Adjusting import settings to get a better fit

In order to adjust the import settings for the motion clip, we need to locate the original FBX file that contains the motion capture data for the walk cycle:

1. In the **Project** panel, expand the PACKT_Animations folder.

2. Select the zombie_walk asset in the **Assets** panel.

   Its import settings will be displayed in the **Inspector** panel.

3. Click the **Animations** tab to view the current import settings.

The initial zwalk01 clip works fine for the male zombie, so we do not want to make any changes directly to this, so instead, we will create a new clip. This will allow us to tailor the sequence to the zombie_f character.

Creating a duplicate walk cycle

If we simply duplicate the animation asset in the **Assets** panel, we would lose the ability to adjust the motion clip's parameters. Making these changes in the root asset from which the clip is derived gives us much more control over the resulting clip:

1. In the **Inspector** panel, click the **+** symbol at the bottom of the **Clips** group to create a new clip.

2. Name the clip `zwalk01f` in the name field.

3. Click the **Clamp Range** button to limit the frame range that the new clip will use.

4. Set the **Start** and **End** frames of the clip to `180` and `225` to match the parameters of `zwalk01`.

5. Click the **Apply** button to save the changes to the asset.

6. Switch to the **Animator** tab and replace the walk cycle in the state machine by clicking the **Walk** state and dragging the `zwalk01f` clip into the motion clip field in the **Inspector** panel.

At this point there should not be any noticeable changes, but replacing the clip in the state machine will allow us to visualize the new clip in the scene.

The next step will be to adjust the animation's height so that the character appears to walk on the floor.

Adjusting the motion parameters

The animation import settings will allow us to make changes to the way the animation data is interpreted to better suit the target character:

1. In the **Assets** panel, click `zombie_walk` to view the parameters in the **Inspector** panel.

2. Make sure that the **Animations** tab is selected and `zwalk01f` is highlighted in the **Clips** box.

3. Check the checkboxes for **Loop Time** and then **Loop Pose** to make sure the sequence cycles smoothly.

4. Scroll down to the **Root Transform Position (Y)** group. This is used to adjust the root height of the model when the motion clip is played.

5. Check the **Bake into Pose** checkbox.

6. Set the **Offset** value to `0.08`.

7. Scroll to the bottom of the **Inspector** panel and click the **Apply** button.

You should notice the character drop slightly in the **Animation Preview** panel at the bottom of the **Inspector** panel.

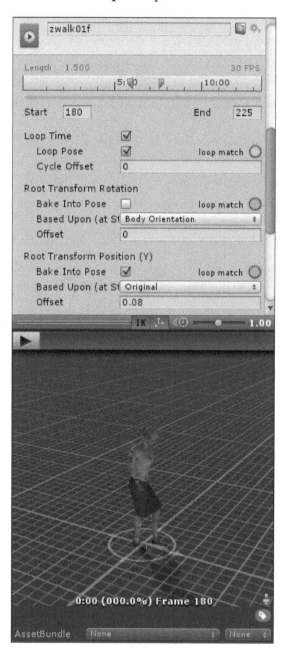

To get a better visualization of the offset, you can orbit the character in the **Animation Preview** panel by dragging within it.

If you need to scale up the panel, drag the gray title bar of the **Animation Preview** up to increase the panel's height within the **Inspector** panel, or drag the entire **Inspector** panel into the center of the interface to undock it.

8. Preview the adjusted motion clip by clicking the **Play** button in the main Unity interface:

9. Check the position of the feet at various stages of the walk cycle using the **Pause** button and adjust the **Offset** value if necessary.

To fix the relative height of the motion clip, we adjusted the **Root Transform Position (Y)** import setting.

There are also options to fix the **XZ** position and the rotation of the animation. In this case, we did not need to adjust these parameters, but they are useful when the root joint has not been centered to the world or faces a different direction than the rigged character model that it is being applied to.

In the **Root Transform Position (Y)** group, we left **Bake Into Pose** unchecked. Checking this will apply the offset to the animation's root joint in its starting pose rather than recalculating it throughout the sequence.

We left **Based Upon (at Start)** to its default value of **Original**. This applies **Offset** to the position of the root joint at the start of the whole imported sequence. Setting this to **Center of Mass** or **Feet** using the dropdown will have different effects. **Center of Mass** will apply the offset to a point equal to half the height of the animation rig.

These parameters are useful when we are working with animation from multiple sources.

Our next objective is to adjust the joint rotation limits to prevent the character's arms from intersecting with her torso. We will achieve this in the next step by adjusting the muscle limits.

Adjusting the muscle limits

With muscle limits, we can define a joint's range of movement and therefore how the character will interpret the animation:

We are covering muscle limits in this chapter because of their relevance to motion capture and retargeting. If you are creating animation sequences specifically for a single character, adjusting muscle limits is as unnecessary as retargeting.

1. In the **Project** panel, locate the FBX_Imports folder and click it to view its contents in the **Assets** panel.

2. Click the zombie_f asset.

   This is the asset used in the zombie_f prefab in our scene. Making changes to the original item will automatically be transferred to the prefab.

   The zombie_f asset's parameters should now be visible in the **Inspector** panel.

3. Click to select the **Rig** tab.

4. Click the **Configure** button.

   At this point, you may be prompted to save the scene. In this case, it is an unnecessary step, as all of the changes so far have been made to prefabs and are already saved at the project level.

   The **Inspector** panel will now display the **Avatar Mapping Definition** panel, where we defined the hierarchy of bones that make up the character's skeleton previously.

5. Click the **Muscles** tab.

A number of muscle limit sliders will appear in the **Inspector** panel, and the character will snap into a test pose in the **Scene** view:

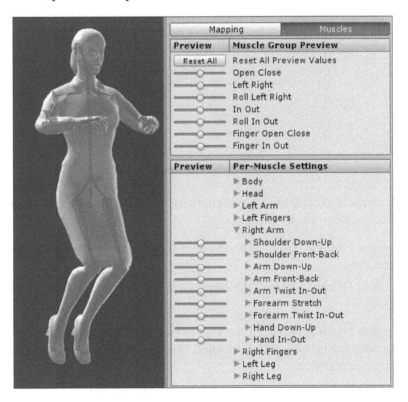

The sliders in the **Muscle Group Preview** box are for testing. Dragging sliders will preview the character Avatar's current muscle limits in the **Scene** view. We will be making changes to the character's muscle limits in the second box, which defines the **Per-Muscle Settings**.

We will start with the right arm, which intersects with the torso during the walk cycle:

1. Click **Right Arm** in the **Per-Muscle Settings** list to view its muscle limit parameters.

2. In the list of parameters that appear beneath **Right Arm**, click **Arm Down-Up** to view its limits slider:

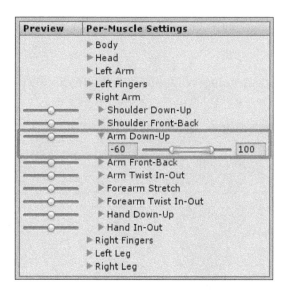

The range of **Arm Down-Up** is currently set with a lower limit of -60 degrees and an upper limit of 100 degrees.

3. Drag the **Preview** slider on the left to visualize this with the character in the **Scene** view.

   It should be apparent that the upper arm is rotating much further than it should.

4. Drag the **Preview** slider all the way to the right and adjust the upper limit to restrict the movement of the joint. A value of around 80 should allow enough movement.

5. Drag the **Preview** slider all the way to the left and adjust the muscle's lower limit. The joint should stop rotating when it starts to intersect with the torso. A value of -41 should work for this.

6. Click the **Apply** button to store the changes:

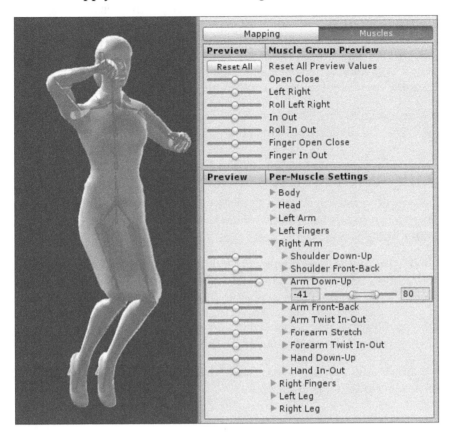

7. Repeat this process for the muscle limits in the **Left Arm**.

8. Make sure to click the **Apply** button to save your changes.

9. In the **Right Arm** list, select **Forearm Stretch**.

    Dragging the **Preview** slider for this muscle limit should show that the forearm intersects with the upper arm at its lower limit.

10. Move the lower limit further towards the center of the scale, or type in a new number so that the forearm no longer intersects with the upper arm. A value of -65 should work pretty well.

    In this case, it is not necessary to adjust the upper limit as the rotation comes to an end when the arm is straight.

11. Repeat these changes in the **Forearm Stretch** parameter for the **Left Arm**.

Test more of the **Preview** sliders to see whether it is necessary to make more changes to the muscle limits. Remember this is only necessary if there is a conflict in the rotation of the joints in the animation sequence we are using, or if you want to add distinct characteristics to the animation when played with a particular character.

Different clothing, such as the female zombie's skirt and heels, could be factors that would limit the rotation of joints and ultimately how the character moves.

Another Mecanim tool that can be used to adapt motion sequences in Unity is the body mask. We will demonstrate this next with the male zombie character.

Working with Avatar Body Masks

As well as adapting motion sequences to specific character types with muscle limit definitions, Mecanim has the ability to blend together parts of different sequences using **Avatar Body Masks**.

Much like masks used to hide portions of still images in image-editing software such as Photoshop, Mecanim's body masks can be used to hide parts of a character animation allowing motion in an underlying layer to become visible.

This can be useful when it is necessary to add subtle differences to recurring animation sequences such as those used by the zombie enemies in this example.

In this section we will add an Avatar Body Mask and use it on the prefab male zombie character to vary his animation.

Opening the new scene

The assets needed to demonstrate body masks have been put together in a scene.

Open the scene Chapter5_2. This scene contains the conference room environment, along with the zombie_m character already set up with an animator controller and a script to enable him to switch between states.

If you test the game at this point, by pressing the **Play** button, you will see the zombie idle for a while before starting his walk animation:

In the next step we will create our first mask:

1. In the **Project** panel, select and expand the PACKT_Masks folder.
2. To create the new mask asset, right-click in the **Assets** panel and choose **Create | Avatar Mask**.
3. When the icon for the mask appears in the folder, rename this z_Legs.

4. Click to expand the **Humanoid** parameter in the **Inspector** panel.

The mask diagram will appear in the **Inspector** panel.

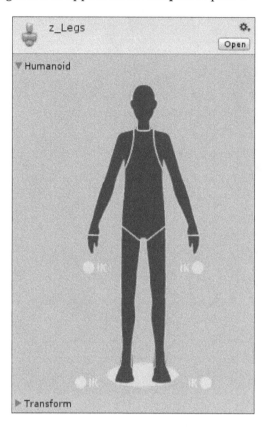

The mask diagram is similar to the **Avatar Definition** map in which we defined the bone positions within the rigged character model in the **Import** settings.

In this case, the diagram is used to specify which parts of the animation will be masked. By default nothing is masked. You can click on each part of the body to remove it (or mask it out).

Avatar mask options are:

- **Head**
- **Right Arm**
- **Left Arm**
- **Right Hand**
- **Left Hand**

- ° **Torso**
- ° **Right Leg**
- ° **Left Leg**
- ° **Root**
- ° **Right Arm IK**
- ° **Left Arm IK**
- ° **Right Leg IK**
- ° **Left Leg IK**

The root is denoted by the circle at the feet of the character in the diagram. The **IK** masks will cause the arm or leg's motion to be driven by the hand or foot respectively.

5. Now, click on all of the areas except for the right and left legs.

   The areas that you have clicked will turn red in the diagram:

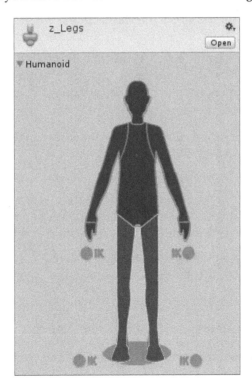

In the next stage we will be creating a new animation layer within the character's animator controller. Only the areas that are green in the diagram will run the new animation, the rest of the areas will use the controller's base layer of animation.

Using this technique, parts of different animation sequences can be put together to create composite motion clips. The animator needs more than one layer to use a mask. We will create this in the next step.

Creating a second layer in the animator controller

Multiple layers can be added to an animator controller, enabling parts of different motion clips to be masked together. In this step we will add a second layer to the controller:

1. If it is not already selected, use the **Hierarchy** panel to select the **zombie_m** game object.

2. In the top-center of the Unity interface, click the **Animator** tab to open the **Animator** panel.

    By default, the controller's states and transitions are grouped in the base layer, but we will create a new layer to house the masking to enable the animation to happen at the same time without affecting the other parts of the skeleton.

3. Create the new layer by clicking on the + symbol in the **Layers** tab in the top-left corner of the **Animator** panel.

4. Rename the new layer **Legs**.

5. Click on the **Legs** layer in the **Animator** window. It will replace the base layer within the interface and appear as a default animation controller window with the two default states — **Any State** and **Entry**.

6. Click the settings icon on the right of the **Legs** layer tab.

    This will allow you to adjust settings associated with the layer.

7. Drag the **Weight** slider to its maximum value, 1.

    This value defines the strength of the animation that will mask the original.

8. Click the radio button next to the **Mask** field and choose the z_Legs mask in the dialogue that appears.

In the **Legs** layer we will define the motion sequence that will replace that in the base layer:

We next need to define the states and transitions as we would usually do in an animator controller.

Creating states in the mask layer

States in a mask layer typically define when the layer is used:

1. Create a new state within the **Animator** panel by right-clicking and selecting **Create State | Empty**.

2. Click on the new state to open its properties within the **Inspector** panel.

3. Rename the new state null state.

   The null state is the default state for the layer. It does not need a motion added to it because the base layer's animation will be visible when the null state is active.

4. Create a second state.

5. Rename the new state AltWalk.

6. In the **Project** panel, open the PACKT_Animations folder.

7. Drag the z_walk02 animation into the motion slot in the **Inspector** panel, this will define the replacement animation that will be used just for the legs.

Setting the parameter and transitions in the mask layer

Just like the base layer, the **Leg** layer needs a parameter and transitions to effect its states:

1. Create a new parameter by clicking the **+** symbol in the **Parameters** box in the lower left of the **Animator** window.

2. Choose **Bool** as the parameter type.

3. Rename the parameter `AltWalking`. Leave its checkbox unchecked.

4. Click **null State** and select **Make Transition**.

5. Click **AltWalk** to select it as the target state for the transition.

6. Click the transition to expose its properties within the **Inspector** panel.

7. In the **Conditions** group, choose `AltWalking` from the drop-down list.

8. Its case should be left to `true`.

9. Create a second transition to link the **AltWalk** state back to the **null State**.

10. Once again choose `AltWalking` as the condition, but this time choose **false** as the case.

That is it for the animator, but by default the secondary layer will not come into play, it needs to be set up within the character's animation script.

Editing the script

Now we will edit the script to activate the mask layer:

1. In the **Project** panel, click the `PACKT_Scripts` folder to view its contents in the **Assets** panel.

2. Double-click `zombie_m_idleWalk` to open it in MonoDevelop.

3. Add the following variable to the others near the top of the script:

    ```
    var changeWalk : boolean = false;
    ```

    This boolean will allow us to change the Mecanim parameter in the script.

4. Add the following code to the top of the `Update` function:

    ```
    theAnimator.SetBool("AltWalking",changeWalk);

    if(Input.GetKeyDown("b"))
    {
        changeWalk = !changeWalk;
    }
    ```

Firstly, we tie the script boolean `changeWalk` to the Mecanim boolean `AltWalking` in our animator controller.

Next we check for input from the *B* key to switch the boolean case of the `AltWalk` state to `true`, and play the replacement walk animation in the legs.

Previewing the masked animation

We can stop at this point and see what the masked animation currently looks like:

1. Preview the game by pressing the **Play** button in the top center of the interface.

2. After idling for a short time, the character will go into a walk.

3. Press the *B* key to activate the masked layer.

The animation will switch to the alternate clip:

The resulting composite animation uses the `zwalk01` motion derived from the motion capture file, but augments it with the leg animation from `zwalk02`.

Considering that our game will feature a number of enemy characters on the screen at the same time, this technique could be used effectively to give the impression of individuality: making our zombies move differently without the memory overhead involved with creating a different set of animation sequences for each enemy.

In the next section we will further demonstrate these possibilities by creating variations with the two walk cycles.

Creating five walk variations from two walk cycles

As well as correcting motion sequences to get them to fit different characters, Avatar Body Masks can be used to add variety to multiple characters that use the same initial model.

In *Chapter 4, Working with Motion Capture Data*, we created two unique walk cycles from a single motion capture sequence. In the next step we will further vary these by masking the head, arms, and legs from each sequence:

1. In the Unity project, open the scene Chapter5_3.

   The scene is the same simple room interior, but this time containing five identical male zombies.

   Currently each of the zombie characters shares the same animator controller. It is set up to play the same walk sequence after idling for a short time.

2. In the top-center of the Unity interface, press the **Play** button to preview the walk animation:

As the zombie characters all begin walking at the same time, the uniformity of their animation sequence is quite obvious.

Mecanim's animation masking tools give us some more options.

Adding more Avatar masks

In the last section, we used a mask to blend in a different leg animation. Here we will create more Avatar masks to use the two walk sequences together to create more variations:

1. In the **Project** panel, click the PACKT_Masks folder to view its contents in the **Assets** panel.

   The folder contains two additional Avatar Masks: z_Arms and z_HeadChestHands.

2. Select the new masks one at a time by clicking them in the **Assets** panel to see how they are set up:
   - For z_Arms only, the arms and hands are highlighted in green
   - For z_HeadChestHands, everything except the head, chest, and hands are masked

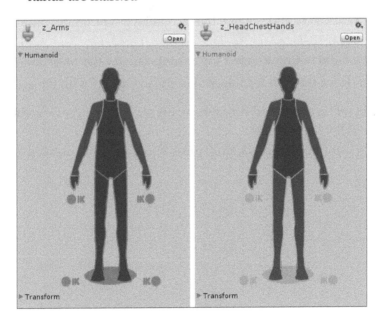

In order to vary the animation masking for each zombie, we need to set each one up with its own animator controller.

3. Click the `PACKT_Controllers` folder in the **Project** panel.

4. Select the asset `ch5_3_1` and duplicate it using the keyboard shortcut *Ctrl + D* (*Cmd + D* if working on a Mac).

5. Select `zombie_m2` in the **Hierarchy** panel.

6. Drag the controller `ch5_3_2` into the **Controller** field beneath the **Animator** component in the **Inspector** panel.

7. Repeat this process for the remaining three instances of the male zombie, giving each a unique animator controller.

8. Select `zombie_m1` in the **Hierarchy** panel.

9. Click the **Animator** tab to view its animator controller.

10. In the **Animator** panel, remove the **Legs** layer by right-clicking it and selecting **Delete**.

11. Select `zombie_m2`.

12. Remove the **Legs** layer in this controller, and replace the motion contained in the **Walk** state, in the character's base layer with `zwalk02`.

13. Select `zombie_m3`.

14. Rename the second layer `Arms` and use the radio button to replace the `z_Legs` mask with `z_Arms` from the selection list.

15. Select `zombie_m4` and rename the second layer within its controller `HeadChestHands`.

16. Use the radio button to select the appropriate Avatar mask asset.

   We can leave the fifth zombie as it is already set up with the `z_Legs` mask.

17. When you have finished configuring the controllers, preview the game by pressing the **Play** button.

18. Once the zombies start walking, press *B* to trigger the masked layers.

The result should be five unique walk cycles using just two animation sequences:

Summary

In this chapter, we demonstrated key animation retargeting using some of the more advanced settings within Mecanim.

We started by demonstrating some of the adjustments that can be made to an animation clip using the import settings.

Next, we looked at the **Muscle** tab, showing the limits that can be adjusted to adapt animation sequences to different character types.

We introduced the Avatar Body Mask as a technique to correct and combine different animations and make them more appropriate for individual characters.

Finally, we used this process to add variety to our male zombie character model by creating composite walk cycles from the two sequences created from motion capture data in *Chapter 4, Working with Motion Capture Data*.

In the next chapter, we will take a closer look at Mecanim's support for facial animation, and how a simple face motion clip can be used with audio to create a dramatic moment in our game.

6
Talking Heads

In this chapter, we will demonstrate the implementation of basic facial animation with Mecanim. Mecanim's **Humanoid** animation type has a small predefined set of bones that will accommodate face animation. This can be layered within the animator controller, effectively separating body and face animation to be triggered under different conditions.

There are several valid reasons due to which we may want to separate out face and body animations — we want the player to be given a sign that the enemy has spotted them. We do not have a way of determining what state the enemy character is in when they spot the player. We do not want them to immediately attack, however, we want to give the player an opportunity to react before the enemy. After all, the enemy is a slow moving zombie.

In this chapter, you will be:

- Preparing conditions in the scene to allow a triggered response
- Updating the zombie's script to allow it to target and move toward the player
- Implementing an audio asset using a component and the script
- Adding the face skeletal animation to the animator in its own masked layer
- Controlling a blendshape animation in the animator
- Controlling the zombie's turn and add further animation
- Splitting behavior into self-contained functions within the script
- Accurately synchronizing the sound using an animation event

We will start by demonstrating the existing simple behavior with the female zombie character and simple room environment both introduced previously.

Adding the snarl face animation to the female zombie character

Before we get to grips with the animator controller and the script, let's take a look at the scene and run through the zombie's current behavior. The environment is the simple conference room used in *Chapter 5, Retargeting Animation*.

Setting the scene in Unity

Our starting scene includes the conference room environment, the first person controller and a single enemy — the female zombie introduced in *Chapter 2, Rigging Characters for Unity in 3ds Max and Maya*.

1. Open the scene `Chapter6_Start` within the Unity project.
2. Preview the scene by pressing the **Play** button in the top center of the Unity interface.

With the first-person controller, we can navigate through the space toward the enemy.

The female zombie idles for a while before walking forward. At the moment, we can get close to the zombie without seeing any kind of change in its behavior.

We will add some basic functionality to the script to lay the groundwork for our snarl animation as a response to the player's movement.

Adding code to the zombie_ready script

The script currently attached to the female zombie, adequately handles its current states: **Idle** and **Walk**. We need to add a few lines of code to the script to trigger the face animation:

1. In the **Project** panel, scroll down until the `PACKT_Scripts` folder is visible.
2. Double-click on it to make its contents visible in the **Assets** panel.
3. Locate `zombie_ready` and double-click on it to open the script in MonoDevelop.

We will start by adding a few variables. At the top of the script, add the following lines of code:

```
var target : Transform;
var alerted : boolean = false;
var snarlSound : AudioClip;
var soundReady : boolean = true;
```

The `target` variable will store the player character's position. The next variable, `alerted` is a boolean. It is basically an on/off switch that will allow the zombie to go into a new routine.

The next two variables deal with the sound that we will be using to make it clear that the zombie has been alerted.

The `snarlSound` variable is an audio clip that will store the actual sound, and `soundReady` is a boolean that will be used to prevent the sound playing more than once.

By default `alerted` is set to `false`, but we will switch it to `true` in the next few lines of code.

Add the following code within the `Update` function:

```
if(Input.GetButton("Fire1") && alerted == false)
{
    alerted = true;
}

if(alerted)
{
    TurnToPlayer();
}
```

Here, we use the player input (in this case, the **Fire1** button) to trigger the boolean switch. This is a temporary measure—triggers and ranges are covered fully in *Chapter 9, Controlling Enemy Animation with AI and Triggers*.

The advantage in testing the boolean switch with player input, at this stage, is that it allows us to make sure that the boolean is working before we further complicate the script.

We also have an `if` statement to check whether the boolean has been switched on, this in turn runs the `TurnToPlayer` function, which we will look at next.

Adding the TurnToPlayer function

Instead of continuing to add code in the Update function, we separate out the actual behavior into a new custom function named TurnToPlayer.

Separating these commands makes our script easier to read, it also allows for a variety of ways to call the function—imagine that our player character has triggered an alarm, which causes all of the enemies in the level to become aware of him and turn toward him.

Add the following code to the bottom of the script:

```
function TurnToPlayer()
{
    transform.LookAt(target);
    yield WaitForSeconds(2);

    if(soundReady)
    {
        GetComponent.<AudioSource>().PlayOneShot(snarlSound);
        soundReady = false;
    }
    Walks();
}
```

The first command makes the zombie turn to face the player. We create a short pause with the yield WaitForSeconds method, we then check to see if the soundReady boolean variable is true and then play our audio. The zombie will then go into the Walks function, which has already been defined in the script.

Save the script and minimize MonoDevelop. If you preview the scene in the **Game** view, there will not be any noticeable change to the zombie's behavior.

Despite the fact that you can switch the alerted boolean on (it will be visible in the **Inspector** panel) by pressing the **Fire1** button (set by default to the left mouse button), the zombie will not turn toward the player as the player's **Transform** has not yet been defined as the target.

We can take care of that next.

Connecting the variables in the Inspector panel

Variables can often be defined completely within the script, but Unity's drag-and-drop functionality makes connecting variables extremely quick and easy.

First, we will define the player as the target:

1. Make sure that the `zombie_f` game object is selected in the **Hierarchy** panel—its components should appear in the **Inspector** panel. If necessary, scroll down until all of the `zombie_ready` script's variables are visible.

2. Drag the `FPSController` game object from the **Hierarchy** panel into the target variable slot.

3. In the **Project** panel, click on the `PACKT_Sounds` folder to view its contents in the **Assets** panel.

4. Drag `zombie_growl` into the **snarlSound** slot in the **Inspector** panel.

   In order to play sound, game objects need to have an audio source component attached to them.

5. Add the **Audio Source** component from the **Component** tab in the menu bar at the top of the Unity interface by navigating to **Component | Audio | Audio Source**.

It is not necessary to specify the file within the **Audio Source** component, as we have already taken care of that in the script.

Additionally, when game objects have more than one sound to play, it is preferable to define the audio clip in the script rather than the component.

Both the target and sound variables have now been defined, and there should be some noticeable changes when the game is previewed:

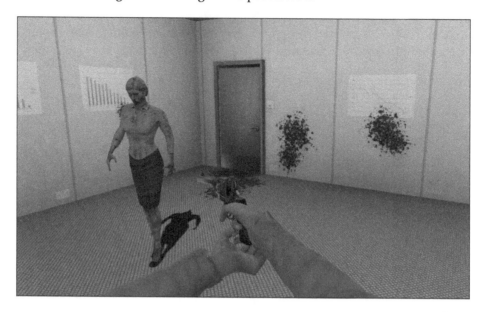

The zombie will idle for a short time before starting her walk cycle as before. This time, when the fire button is pressed, she will walk toward the player and the snarl sound should play.

Now that we have set up some basic behavior, we just need to make a few changes to the animator controller in order to see our face animation in the game.

Updating the animator controller to include the face animation

In the previous chapter, we created masks for various parts of the body to add variation to our stock animation sequences. The animator controller connected to the zombie in our current scene is set up the same way, there are just a few changes that need to be made:

1. Click on the zombie_f game object in the **Hierarchy** panel to select it.
2. Click on the **Animator** tab in the top center of the Unity interface to switch to the **Animator** panel.
3. In the top left of the **Animator** panel, click on the **Layers** tab to activate it.

The zombie's animator controller consists of a base layer containing two states: **Idle** and **Walk**. We need to create a new layer for the face animation:

1. In the top left of the **Animator** panel, click on the **+** symbol in the **Layers** tab to create a new layer.

2. Rename the layer `Face`.

3. Set the layer's **Weight** field to `1`.

4. In the new **Face** layer, click on the radio button next to the **Mask** field and select `z_Head` from the list.

5. Leave the **Blending** type set to its default value of `Override`.

Refer to the following screenshot:

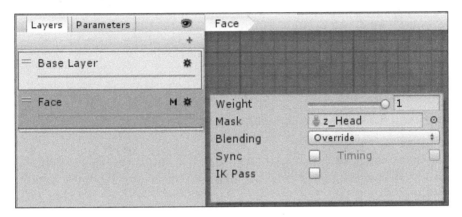

Next, we need to create a new state to contain our snarl animation.

Adding the Snarl state

We have set up states manually in previous chapters, but if you know exactly which animation you want a state to use, you can also just drag the motion clip into the **Animator** panel:

1. In the **Project** panel, select the `PACKT_Animations` folder.

2. When its contents appear in the **Assets** panel, scroll down to locate `zombie_snarl`.

3. Click on the small arrow next to its name to view the contained assets.

4. Drag the animation file named `snarl` into an empty area of the **Animator** panel.

    A new state will be created with the same name as the motion clip that it contains.

5. In the **Inspector** panel, capitalize the first letter of the state's name to keep it consistent with the other states on the animator controller's base layer.

Unless we want the **Snarl** state to be constantly active, we will need to set up a **Null** state in the same layer.

Creating a Null state

As the **Face** layer is constantly active, we need to create a blank state that will be in effect whenever we do not want to see the zombie's snarl:

1. Right-click on a blank area of the **Animator** panel.
2. Navigate to **Create State | Empty**.
3. In the **Inspector** panel, rename the state `Null`.

    Leaving the state's motion field empty will ensure that the base layer's current motion clip will be fully visible.

    Because we created the **Snarl** layer first, it is automatically the default layer and will run without being prompted. We can fix this by making **Null** the default state.

4. Right-click on **Null** in the **Animator** window.
5. Choose **Set As Layer Default State** from the list.

The **Null** state will turn orange, indicating that it is now the default:

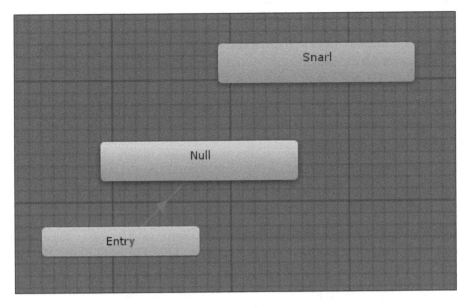

Next, we need to connect the layer's two states with transitions.

Setting transitions between the Null and Snarl states

In real-world terms, we want the snarl to happen regardless of whether the zombie is idling, walking, or lying on the ground. Having created the two states, we connect them with **to** and **return** transitions:

1. Create a transition by right-clicking on **Null** and choosing **Make Transition**.

2. Click on the **Snarl** state to terminate the transition.

3. Use the same process to create the **return** transition from **Snarl** to **Null**.

Next, we will create a parameter for the **Snarl** state that will allow it to run.

Creating the IsSnarling parameter

The parameter required by the transition will be set within our `zombie_ready` script:

1. Click on the **+** symbol in the **Parameters** box in the lower left of the **Animator** panel.

2. Choose a **Trigger** type parameter and rename it `IsSnarling`.

3. Leave the new parameter's radio button in its deactivated state, so the snarl animation does not override the original head animation by default.

4. Click on the transition to select it.

5. In the **Inspector** panel, locate the **Conditions** box and click on the drop down.

6. Choose `IsSnarling` as the condition.

We can leave the return transition with its default settings. The `Exit Time` condition will wait for the snarling motion to play through before returning to the **Null** state.

At this point, we will want to make a few small edits to our script to make sure that the **Face** layer works correctly.

Editing the script to include the Face layer

Next, we will make some additions to the existing functions to make sure that the **Face** layer becomes active during gameplay:

1. Edit the `TurnToPlayer` function to set the `IsSnarling` trigger:

```
function TurnToPlayer()
{
    transform.LookAt(target);
    yield WaitForSeconds(2);
    if(soundReady)
    {
        theAnimator.SetTrigger("IsSnarling");
    GetComponent.<AudioSource>().PlayOneShot(snarlSound);
        soundReady = false;
    }
    Walks();
}
```

Here, we tie the `IsSnarling` Mecanim trigger to the `soundReady` boolean that already exists within this script.

The `soundReady` variable is set up to only be active once, so this is a great way to ensure that our animation only plays one time as well.

2. Save the script.

3. Preview the game by pressing the **Play** button in the top center of the Unity interface.

4. Move the `FPSController` game object close to the female zombie.

5. Click on the left mouse button to switch the zombie's behavior.

The female zombie should turn toward the player and the snarl animation will play:

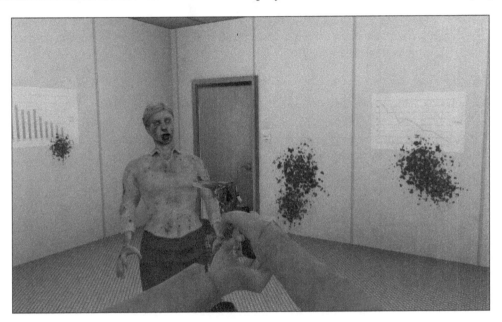

Next, we will make some further improvements to the zombie's behavior by smoothing its rotation.

Smoothing the zombie's turn rotation

The zombie is currently set up to turn to face the player once they have been alerted. The script uses the `transform.LookAt` method, which has an instantaneous effect. We need to adjust the script so that the zombie gradually and naturalistically turns:

1. Back in MonoDevelop, add the following variables near the top of the `zombie_ready` script:

   ```
   var turnSpeed : float = 60.0;
   var turning : boolean = false;
   var angle : float;
   ```

   Here we are defining `turnSpeed`, which is the rate of the zombie's turn. The boolean variable `turning` will be used to play a turning animation while she rotates.

   Lastly, the variable `angle` is used to determine the amount of rotation that the zombie needs to execute.

2. Scroll down to the `TurnToPlayer` function.

3. Replace the function's entire content with the following code:

   ```
   var localRotate =
   transform.InverseTransformPoint(target.position);
   angle = Mathf.Atan2 (localRotate.x, localRotate.z) *
   Mathf.Rad2Deg;
   var maxRotation = turnSpeed * Time.deltaTime;
   var turnAngle = Mathf.Clamp(angle, -maxRotation,
   maxRotation);
   transform.Rotate(0, turnAngle, 0);
   return angle;
   ```

   The first line of the function calculates the relative angle difference between the zombie game object's `transform` and the target's position, storing this as a local `Vector3` variable called `localRotate`.

   The variable `angle`, defined at the top of the script is defined as the sum of `Mathf.Atan2`, which is a calculation along the same lines as `transform.LookAt`.

   The next line defines a local variable named `maxRotation`, which is equal to `turnSpeed` multiplied by `Time.deltaTime`. The `deltaTime` object is time in seconds rather than elapsed frames.

A third local variable, called `turnAngle`, clamps the `angle` variable, keeping it within the value of `maxRotation` so that the zombie does not rotate faster than `turnSpeed`.

The next line of code actually rotates the zombie's `transform` by the value defined by `turnAngle`. The rotation only happens on the *y* axis. The `Rotate` values of **X** and **Z** are set to `0`.

Finally, the variable `angle` is returned, allowing us to use it elsewhere in the script.

4. Save the script.

5. Preview the result by pressing the **Play** button.

When the **Fire1** button is pressed, the zombie will now rotate smoothly toward the player before walking toward him.

At the moment, the `Snarl` animation will not play, nor does the audio, because we deleted the code when we updated the `TurnToPlayer` function.

Before we add this back in, we will add some animation for the zombie's turn.

Implementing the turn animation

In this case, there is a single animation sequence that will be played when the zombie is turning to the right or left.

The FBX file containing the animation has already been imported. The next step is to add the resulting motion clip to the animator controller in its own state.

Adding the turning state

The turn animation is a single looping sequence used for a left or right turn:

1. Make sure that the **Animator** panel is visible and the base layer is active.

2. In the **Project** panel, locate the `PACKT_Animations` folder and click on it once to view its contents in the **Assets** panel.

3. Locate the `zombie_turn` asset and expand its hierarchy by clicking on the arrow next to its name.

4. Drag the `zombie_turn` animation into a blank area of the **Animator** panel to create a new state containing the clip.

5. In the **Inspector** panel, rename the state `Turn`:

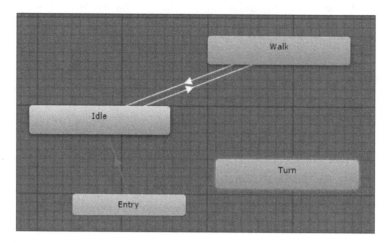

Next, we will set up an appropriate parameter and create transitions to and from our existing states.

Setting up the IsTurning parameter

We want the `zombie_turn01` animation to play only when the zombie is turning toward the player, so we can use a boolean parameter which can be easily switched on and off in the script:

1. In the **Parameters** box, click on the + symbol to create a new parameter and choose `Bool` as the type.

2. Rename the parameter `IsTurning` and leave it unchecked.

We will use this parameter as a condition to allow us to transition to the `Turn` state.

Creating the transitions to connect the turning state

The transitions will connect **Turn** to our existing states using the IsTurning parameter as the condition:

1. Right-click on the **Idle** state.

2. Choose **Make Transition** and click on the **Turn** state to complete the transition.

3. Create the return transition by right-clicking on **Turn** and then clicking on **Idle** to specify it as the end state.

The last step will complete our turn state in the animator controller.

Setting the transitions for the Turn state

The transitions that we have just set up require **Conditions** to enable the state change:

1. Click on the transition connecting **Idle** to **Turn** to view its properties in the **Inspector** panel.

2. In the **Conditions** box, set the parameter to IsTurning by selecting it from the drop-down list.

3. Make sure that the conditional is set to true.

4. For the return transition, choose the IsTurning parameter once again, but this time, set its conditional to False.

5. Repeat this process for both of the transitions linking **Turn** to **Walk** state.

6. Add an extra condition for the return transition to **Walk** specifying IsWalking as the parameter and True as the conditional.

7. Add a condition for the **Walk** to **Turn** transition, choosing IsWalking as the parameter and false as the conditional.

This will ensure that the zombie is not trying to walk and turn at the same time.

Next, we will return to MonoDevelop to update our script to accommodate the state.

Updating the zombie_ready script to accommodate the Turn state

The script currently allows the zombie to rotate smoothly toward the player when he is targeted, but switching the animation states appropriately necessitates just a little more code:

1. If it is not already open, double-click on `zombie_ready` in the **Assets** panel to initialize it in MonoDevelop.

2. At the top of the `Update` function, add the following line of code:

   ```
   theAnimator.SetBool("IsTurning", turning);
   ```

   This ties our Mecanim Bool parameter `IsTurning` to the boolean variable `turning` that we just added.

   When we updated this script previously, we made the `TurnToPlayer` function return a variable named `angle` that is stored as a public variable in the script.

   We will make use of this variable to get our turn animation playing.

3. In MonoDevelop, locate the second `if` statement in the `Update` function.

   It should currently look like this:

   ```
   if(alerted)
   {
       TurnToPlayer();
   }
   ```

   As soon as the zombie is alerted (by the **Fire1** button), the `TurnToPlayer` function is run.

4. Add the following code inside the `if(alerted)` statement:

   ```
   if(angle > 5 ||angle < -5)
   {
       turning = true;
   }
   ```

   This further nested `if` statement checks whether the angle variable is greater than 5 or less than -5. When one of these conditions is met, then we will allow the turning animation to play.

With less of an angle, the rotation time would be too short resulting in a jumpy and incomplete animated transition.

We can define what happens in this case in the next statement.

5. Add the following code within the `if` statement:

```
else if(angle < 5 && angle > -5)
{
    if(soundReady)
    {
        Snarl();
    }
}
```

If `angle` is sufficiently low, we check to see if the `soundReady` variable is `true`. This boolean is a one shot deal, it never gets reset to `true`, ensuring that our zombie will only snarl once, when it is first alerted by the player.

The snarl animation and sound will be taken care of in the `Snarl` function a little later on.

> Containing pieces of behavior in their own functions like this makes it possible to trigger them with external events. We will cover some examples of this in *Chapter 9, Controlling Enemy Animation with AI and Triggers*.

So, what happens if the snarl animation has already been played? It seems natural for the zombie to move toward the player to attack.

6. Add the following code directly beneath the `else if` statement:

```
else
{
    turning = false;
    WalkTowards();
}
```

The `else` statement directly follows an `if` statement and acts as a catch all.

The finished `Update` function should look like this:

```
function Update()
{
    theAnimator.SetBool("IsTurning", turning);
    if(Input.GetButton("Fire1") && alerted == false)
    {
        alerted = true;
    }
    if(alerted)
    {
        TurnToPlayer();
        if(angle > 5 ||angle < -5)
        {
            turning = true;
        }
        else if(angle < 5 && angle > -5)
        {
            if(soundReady)
            {
                Snarl();
            }
            else
            {
                turning = false;
                WalkTowards();
            }
        }
    }
}
```

Our next step is to add the `WalkTowards` and `Snarl` functions that we already run in this code.

7. Add the following code at the bottom of the script:

```
function WalkTowards()
{
    var direction =
    transform.TransformDirection(Vector3.forward *
    walkSpeed);
    charControl.SimpleMove(direction);
    theAnimator.SetBool("IsWalking", true);
}
```

With our `TurnToPlayer` function, we have already turned the zombie toward the player, so all that is left is to move her forward.

Here, we define a `Vector3` variable named `direction` as `Vector3.forward` (or `positive z`) multiplied by `walkSpeed`. As the zombie has a character controller component, we use the `SimpleMove` method.

We also set the Mecanim variable `IsWalking` to `true`, which will transition into the **Walk** state allowing the appropriate animation to play.

Next, we will get the snarl working again and finish up the script.

Creating the Snarl function

We previously tested the snarl animation, but removed the code when we added complexity to the script. Grouping commands together in a custom function often makes for a cleaner and easier to read script, it also makes it much easier to add further effects.

1. At the end of the script, add the following code:

```
function Snarl()
{
    GetComponent.<AudioSource>().PlayOneShot(snarlSound);
    theAnimator.SetTrigger("IsSnarling");
    soundReady = false;
}
```

2. Save the script.

After we put the audio back in, all we are doing here is setting the Mecanim trigger `IsSnarling` and switching off the `soundReady` boolean to ensure that the animation will not be triggered again.

If we test the game at this point, we should see the zombie transition from the turn animation back into walk whenever the player stays in the same place.

The snarl animation will play once, when the zombie is alerted. Our next objective is to synchronize and adjust the audio to improve the effect in the game.

Synchronizing the snarl sound

Currently, we have the audio set up to play after a certain amount of time, but Unity will allow us to queue it up with our animation sequence more precisely using animation events.

In Unity, an **event** is a marker set at a point within an animation sequence that can send a message to a game object to make something else happen.

For imported animation, like we are using for the characters, events are added to clips when they are defined in the **Import** settings.

1. In the **Project** panel, locate the PACKT_Animations folder and click on it to view its contents in the **Assets** panel.

2. Click on the zombie_snarl asset to view its parameters in the **Inspector** panel.

   When the **Animation** import tab is active, you will see a single clip named Snarl.

3. Scroll to the bottom of the clip's parameters, and the click on the small arrow next to **Events** to view the hidden parameters.

4. Click on the **Add Event** icon.

   A marker will appear on the timeline, and the **Edit Animation Event** dialog will appear over the main Unity interface.

   You can usually drag the time slider in the **Animation Preview** panel to match a specific action in the animation, but as the animation is restricted to the face, we will need to know when the sound should start to play. For this clip, the sound needs to start on frame 10.

   Unfortunately, the events time slider is proportionate, rather than giving us specific frame numbers. However, we can scroll up to the clip time slider, which will let's define the duration in frames.

5. Move the event marker to the appropriate position on the time slider.

   The event can send variables to a game object's script or run a function. In this case, we will set up our audio in its own function named SnarlSound.

6. In the **Edit Animation Event** dialog, enter SnarlSound in the **Function** field.

7. Select the name of the game object that this should be sent to in the **Object** field, by clicking on the radio button and selecting `zombie_f` from the drop-down list:

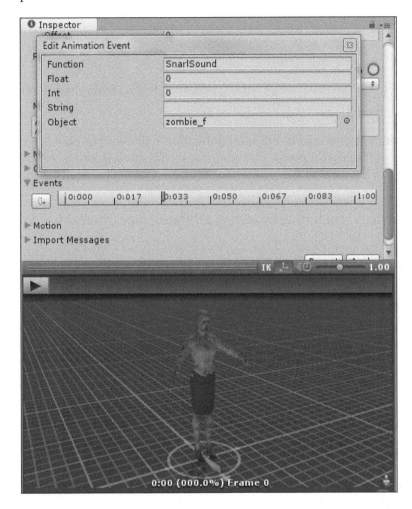

8. Make sure to save the changes to the **Import** settings, by clicking on the **Apply** button located above the **Animation Preview** panel.

Lastly, we need to add the `SnarlSound` function to our script.

9. At the bottom of the script, add the new function:

```
function SnarlSound()
{
    GetComponent.<AudioSource>().PlayOneShot(snarlSound);
    theAnimator.SetBool("IsSnarling",false);
    return;
}
```

10. Delete the `GetComponent.<AudioSource>()` line from the previous function.

11. Save the script.

When the game is previewed, the snarl animation will begin to play, triggering the snarl sound at the correct point. The `SnarlSound` function is triggered externally, from the tag in the motion file. This is an accurate way to sync sounds and other functions.

We can take this a step further by adding a different type of animation to the face.

Driving a blendshape animation with the animator controller

The zombie's face animation is a nice touch, to make it clear to the player that something is happening in the game. The effect is quite subtle; due to the limited number of face bones that we can retarget in the **Humanoid** rig type, we are not able to get a full range of expression across in the zombie's face.

One way to get around this is to use a different kind of animation. **Blendshape** or **Morph Target** animation types do not use bones or joints to deform the model, but use a second, altered version of the mesh. Blendshape animation sequences can be driven in the animator the same way that skeletal animation can.

Blendshape animation sequences are usually unique to a model. They are created by making a copy of the whole or part of a mesh and then moving, scaling, and rotating vertices to change the shape—creating a facial expression or some other kind of deformation.

After the blendshape has been linked to the model, it can be exported in the usual way as an FBX file. The FBX exporter has a **Deformation** section with a checkbox for **Morphs** that needs to be checked to export this feature.

We have a model in the project that has already been set up like this with a blendshape.

Viewing the blendshape in Unity

In this section, we will look at the model and preview the blendshape:

1. In the **Project** panel, select the FBX_Imports folder to view its contents in the **Assets** panel.

2. Locate zombie_f_blend and click on it to view its **Import** settings in the **Inspector** panel.

3. In the **Model** tab, verify that the **Import BlendShapes** checkbox is checked.

   This should be checked by default.

   Unlike skeletal animation, blendshapes cannot be previewed in the **Inspector** panel. We need to do this in the scene.

4. Drag zombie_f_blend into the **Hierarchy** panel to instance it in the scene.

   The zombie will instantiate with a blank material. We can add the correct material next.

5. In the **Project** panel, select the PACKT_Materials folder to view its contents in the **Assets** panel.

6. Locate the zombie_f material and drag this onto the model in the scene view:

Apart from the addition of the blendshape, this character is identical to the model that we have been working with previously. It too has a skeleton that has already been setup to work with Mecanim.

7. In the **Hierarchy** panel, click on the small arrow next to zombie_f_blend, to expand its hierarchy.

8. Click on the zombie_f child object to select it.

    Its settings will appear in the **Inspector** panel.

    At the top of the **Skinned Mesh Renderer** component, there is an expandable section for blendshapes.

9. Click on the small arrow next to **BlendShapes** to expand its parameters.

    The value for zombie_f_snarl is set to 0 by default.

10. Drag on zombie_f_snarl to increase the value.

    You should see the zombie's expression change in the **Scene** view.

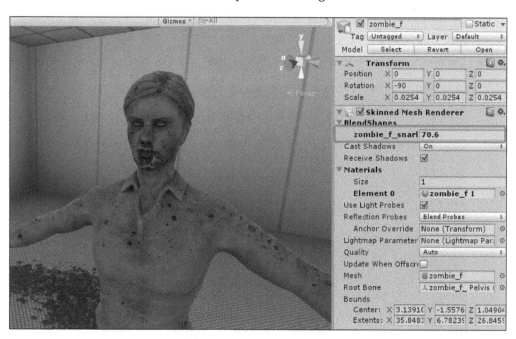

The zombie's eyes will close slightly and her face will contract into an expression. There is little movement in the mouth, as this is still going to be handled by the skeletal animation.

11. Return the `zombie_f_snarl` blendshape value to `0`.

Our next step will help us get the blendshape into the animator.

Keyframing the face blendshape

We have got the face blendshape working, but we still need to set up the timing.

1. In the **Hierarchy** panel, click on the `zombie_f_blend` parent object to select it.

2. At the top of the **Inspector** panel, you should see that the game object's animator component is currently empty.

3. Open the **Animation** window by navigating to **Window** | **Animation**.

    In the center of the **Animation** window, you will see a prompt to create an animation clip for the currently selected object.

    We need to set up an animation sequence for the blendshape to tie the value to a time line.

4. Click on the **Create** button to create an animation clip.

    Another dialog will appear prompting you to select a name and save the location for the new clip.

5. Name the clip `zombie_f_snarlBlend` and save it in the `PACKT_Animations` folder.

    The empty timeline will appear in the **Animation** window. The play/pause control in the main Unity interface will be displayed in red to indicate we are in **Record** mode.

    At the moment, our zombie is half-embedded in the floor. Do not worry about this at the moment.

    Before we start creating keyframes in the timeline, we need to specify a property.

6. Click on the **Add Property** button and select **zombie_f - Skinned Mesh Renderer - BlendShape.zombie_f_snarl** from the expandable list.

7. Click on the small **+** symbol next to this line to select the blendshape as the property we want to animate.

   The start and end keyframes will be created automatically in the timeline:

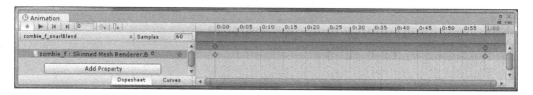

   The blendshape value is set to 0 in both keyframes and the animation is 1 second long.

8. Drag the playhead – the red line on the animation timeline, to frame 30 and create a new keyframe by clicking on the diamond shaped **Add Keyframe** button.

9. Still in the **Animation** window, increase the horizontal size of the **Properties** list by dragging it to the right, so you can see the full name of the blendshape property and the value 0 displayed.

10. Click on the 0 to enter the value field and enter the number 100.

11. Click on the **Play** button in the top left of the animation window to play back the resulting animation.

    The zombie will cycle in and out of the blendshape expression.

    The animation has automatically been saved with the name and location that we already specified. At the moment, the clip does not quite sync up with our skeletal animation.

    The snarl skeletal animation is 45 frames long. At 30 frames a second, this equals one and a half seconds.

12. In the **Animation** window, enter the value 90 in the **Samples** field to increase the timeline.

13. Drag the end keyframe to frame 90.

14. Drag the midpoint keyframe – the point where our blendshape is at its maximum value to frame 45.

15. Create another keyframe at frame 75 and set the blendshape value to 60.

    This will slow down the return to the default facial expression.

16. Click on the **Curves** tab at the bottom of the **Animation** window to see the full curve of the animation:

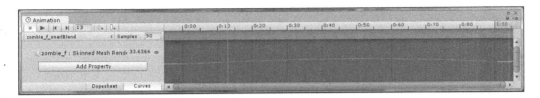

Next, we will set the animation up in the animator controller so that we can view it with the skeletal animation.

17. Add a character controller component and the `zombie_ready` script to the `zombie_f_blend` game object.

A quick way to copy components between game objects while retaining parameters is by right-clicking on the source game object's component. Then, choose **Copy Component** from the drop-down list.

Select the target game object, right-click on the **Inspector** panel and choose **Paste Component** as **New** from the list.

18. Add the `ch6_Start` animator controller by dragging it into the slot near the top of the **Inspector** panel.

In the next step, we will update the animator and add the new blendshape animation.

Updating the animator to handle the blendshape animation

When we added the snarl skeletal animation, we set up a new layer in the animator. We will do something similar for the blendshape animation:

1. In the **Hierarchy** panel, select `zombie_f_blend`.
2. In the **Animator** window, click on the **Layers** tab near the top-left corner.
3. Click on the small **+** symbol to create a new layer.
4. Name the new layer `SnarlBlend`.

5. Click on the small gear icon next to the layer's name to open its properties.

6. Drag the **Weight** value to 1 and set the **Blending** type to Additive.

   Using Additive will allow the blendshape to be used with the skeletal face animation.

7. Making sure that the **SnarlBlend** layer is active, create a new state by right-clicking on an empty area of the graph and navigating to **Choose Create State | Empty**.

8. Select the new state and rename it Null in the **Inspector** panel.

   This is the state that will run when we do not want the blendshape to be in effect.

9. Create a second state and rename it FaceBlend.

10. In the **Project** panel, select the PACKT_Animations folder to view its contents in the **Inspector** panel.

11. Locate the zombie_f_snarlBlend animation clip and drag it into **FaceBlend** state's motion field in the **Inspector** panel.

12. Create transitions between the two states.

13. Assign IsSnarling as the condition for the **Null** to **FaceBlend** transition.

14. Leave the condition blank for the return transition, to allow it to just use Exit Time.

    Our state machine is finished and because we are using an existing parameter, the blendshape will run without any additional code.

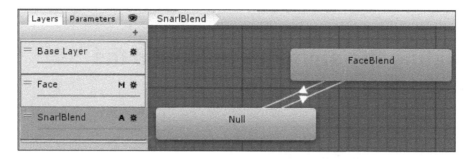

15. Preview the composite animation by pressing the **Play** button in the main Unity interface.

16. Walk close to the female zombie character before pressing the fire button:

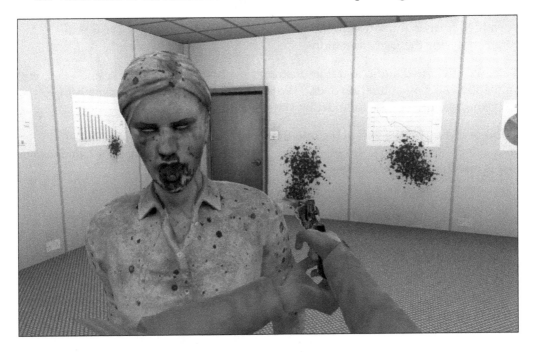

If you completed these steps, the zombie will become alerted, snarl at the player, and walk toward the first-person controller.

At this stage, the zombie does not hurt the player when she reaches them. The zombie's actual attack is covered in depth in *Chapter 9, Controlling Enemy Animation with AI and Triggers.*

Summary

In this chapter, we implemented a layered face animation and added this to the female zombie character's behavior using a script.

We added further animation to the scripted sequence by adding a **Turn** state to better showcase the face animation.

Next, we integrated audio and demonstrated methods of syncing a sound effect with animation using an animation event. We wrapped things up by implementing a blendshape animation in our existing state machine.

In the next chapter, we will delve into the more complex functionality of the animator controller, the seamless blending between the player character animations that is possible with Blend Trees.

7
Controlling Player Animation with Blend Trees

In *Chapter 3*, *Interacting with the Environment*, we introduced the player character model and set up the player's animator controller with a few basic animation sequences. The player can walk, shoot, and pick up items.

The motion sequences were set up in separate states in the controller's base layer to define how the character would transition through its motion sequences. In the transitions that link the states together, we used a Boolean operator to determine when the player would shoot or pick up an item.

In this chapter, we will explore a further level of animation blending within Mecanim. **Blend Trees** are specialized states that can contain many motion sequences.

The use of Blend Trees will add a further level of realism to the game, by blending in subtle animation variations based on the player's input.

In this chapter, you will learn to:

- Implement a Blend Tree to add strafe animation to the existing player character
- Demonstrate the use of parameters, thresholds, and other Blend Tree properties
- Demonstrate the blending of animation sequences driven by player input
- Updating the existing character animation script to be compatible with the Blend Tree

- Use external variables, such as object weight to drive animation blending
- View the Blend Tree in action during play mode

We will start with a simple implementation of a Blend Tree to include variations to the player's idle animation.

Adding a Blend Tree to the player's existing animator controller

We will begin with the player character, which we previously worked with in *Chapter 3, Interacting with the Environment*:

1. Open the `Chapter7_Start` scene in the Unity project.

   The scene contains the `FPSController` prefab, which already has a character controller, animator controller, and a control script attached.

   We will start by testing the controller setup to determine the modifications we are going to make.

2. Preview the game by pressing the **Play** button in the top-center of the unity interface.

When moving from side to side (by pressing the *A* and *S* or the cursor keys), there is no apparent change in the animation.

We will improve this in the next few steps by adding strafing animation, which will add some subtle variation to the character animation when the player moves to the left and right.

Adding strafing animation to the player character with a Blend Tree

We will start by implementing the Blend Tree in the animator controller and making some other small adjustments:

1. In the Unity interface, drag the **Animator** tab toward the top of the screen and release, undocking it from the main interface as a window.

2. Resize the window by dragging the corners until you can comfortably see the current states.

3. Select the **ShootIdle** state.

4. Right-click on and choose **Create new BlendTree in State**.

   In the **Inspector** panel, the existing motion clip will be replaced by the Blend Tree.

   We could also make a Blend Tree as a new state, but we would lose all of our transitions to the other states and have to start from scratch. Converting a state to a Blend Tree will preserve its transitions within the state machine.

5. Double-click on the **ShootIdle** state in the **Animator** window.

   The properties of the Blend Tree will become visible in the **Inspector** panel.

Currently, the Blend Tree does not contain any motion clips. We will explain the properties associated with the Blend Tree before we add the motion clips.

Using Blend Tree properties

The Blend Tree properties in the **Inspector** panel define which motion clips are used and how they are blended together:

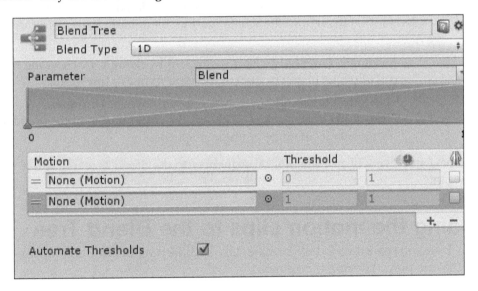

Let's see how to use these properties:

1. In the field at the top is the Blend Tree's name. We will leave it named `Blend Tree` for this example.

2. The **parameter** is chosen from the parameters that you created in the **Animator** window. Only `float` parameters will show up in the drop-down list, as this is the only kind of parameter that the Blend Tree can use.

3. The **blending graph** is a graphic visualization of how the motion clips blend together. Each motion clip is represented as a blue triangle, with the peak representative of the full use of the clip. The blending graph will not be visible until at least two motion fields have been added to the Blend Tree.

4. The **motions** group, contains the motion clips that are usually dragged into the Blend Tree properties from the **Assets** panel.

   Numerous motion clips can be added to each Blend Tree in this way. Alternatively, you can click on the radio button beside the motion field to select a file from a list. You can also add a Blend Tree to a motion field, effectively nesting the Blend Trees.

5. Beside the **Motion** field is the **Threshold** field, which defines where the blended motion fits within the whole motion. By default, these fields are grayed out and inaccessible:

   ° **Automate Thresholds**: This is checked by default. Unchecking this will allow us to access each of the motion field's thresholds.

   ° **Compute Thresholds**: This is visible only when **Automate Thresholds** is unchecked. It allows the computation of the blended clip speeds by average or angular speeds.

In the next step, we will add the motion sequences to the Blend Tree and test it in the game.

Adding the motion clips to the Blend Tree

Blend Trees are specialized kinds of state. Like ordinary states, they contain motion clips that are played during the game:

1. In the **Inspector** panel, click on the + symbol in the **Motion** group.

   This will add a motion slot to the list.

2. Repeat this twice to create three motion fields.

3. In the **Project** panel, navigate to the PACKT_Animations folder and locate the pistolIdles asset.

4. Click on the gray arrow next to the asset's icon to view its contents.

   Three animation files have already been created from the PistolIdles.FBX file.

5. Locate **shootIdle_left** and drag this into the first motion field.

6. Drag **shootIdle** into the second motion field.

7. Drag **shootIdle_right** into the third motion field.

In the **Animator** window, you will see the diagram update to display the Blend Tree's three child nodes:

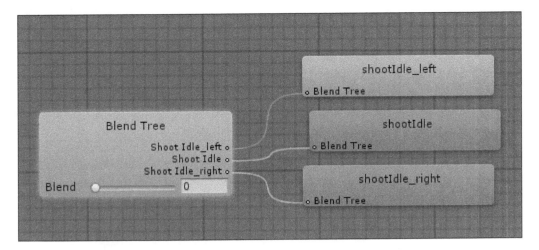

Next, we will set up the parameters that will allow the blending to be implemented.

Adding and adjusting the Blend Tree parameters and thresholds

There are a few more steps that we need to take in order to get the motion clips to play.

Importantly, we have to define a parameter which will enable the blending:

1. Click on the **Parameters** tab in the upper-left of the **Animator** window.
2. Click on the **+** symbol to create a new parameter.
3. Choose **Float** to create a floating point parameter.

   Blend Trees can only use float parameters to blend between motions.

4. Rename the parameter HSpeed.
5. Back in the **Inspector** panel, designate the new parameter for the Blend Tree by clicking on the arrow next to the **Parameter** field and choosing HSpeed.

   Next, we need to set the thresholds for the motion clips to tell Unity when each should be played.

6. Uncheck the **Automate Thresholds** checkbox.

   This will allow us to manually set the thresholds of the three blending motion clips.

7. In the **Threshold** field, next to the **ShootIdle_left** clip, type -1.0.
8. The **shootIdle** state's threshold should be set to 0.0.
9. Leave **shootIdle_right** clip's threshold at its default value of 1.0.

The HSpeed parameter will be driven by the player's horizontal movement input, which we will need to implement in the character script. In Unity, right is positive on the *x* axis, so we define right as 1.0 and left as -1.0.

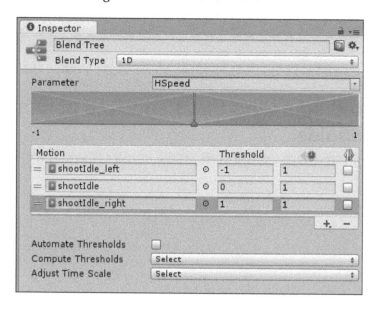

We still need to check for the player's input to blend the animation. We will make some adjustments to our character animation script next.

Updating the character script to use the Blend Tree

Now that we have updated the animator controller, it is necessary to add some code to the script to accommodate the Blend Tree:

1. In the **Project** panel, navigate to the PACKT_Scripts folder.

2. Locate FPSAnimation and double-click on it to open it in MonoDevelop.

3. When the script opens, add the following line of code, following the other variables at the top of the script:

   ```
   var horizontalSpeed : float = 0.0;
   ```

   This float value will be determined by the player's input. In turn, this will be used to control the blending in the animator controller. Setting its value to zero at the start will ensure that this does not happen automatically.

4. Within the Update function add the following lines of code:

   ```
   horizontalSpeed = Input.GetAxis("Horizontal");
   thisAnimator.SetFloat("HSpeed",horizontalSpeed);
   ```

   As we demonstrated previously, the Update function is checked every frame, so it is the ideal place to check for input.

    The same input axis is used to control the player's movement. This is handled in the FPSInputController script that is attached to the FPSController prefab by default.

   Input.GetAxis returns a value between -1 and 1 in float form, based on the left and right movement of the player. By default, the player is moved horizontally with the *A* and *D* keys (also the left and right cursor keys).

   We can simply set our HSpeed Mecanim parameter using this value.

   Now it is time to save our progress and check the results.

5. Save the script and minimize MonoDevelop.

Now that we have set up the float variable and used it to drive a value in the animator controller, we should be able to see a change in the animation states in the game.

Testing the Blend Tree in the Game View

Our Blend Tree should now be implemented in the character. We will test it in the game and make any necessary adjustments:

1. Undock the **Animator** panel or rescale it so that its contents are visible while you test the game.

2. Double-click on the **Idle** state to view the Blend Tree contained within it.

3. Click on the **Game View** tab in the top-center of the main view panel, and make sure the **Maximize on Play** button is not active.

4. Press the **Play** button in the top-center of the Unity interface to preview the game.

5. When *A* or *D* or left and right cursor keys are pressed, there should be a noticeable change in the animation:

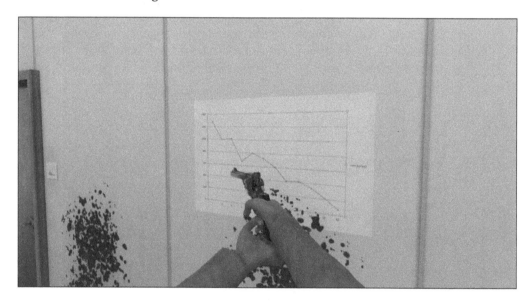

Take a look at the Blend Tree state in the **Animator** window as you move the player character from side to side. The key input smoothly transitions between the three animated sequences:

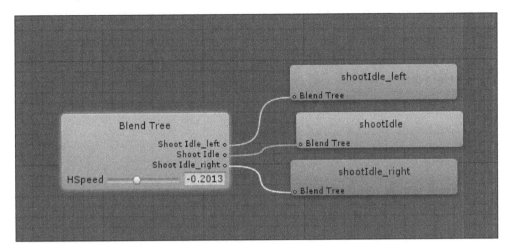

In the next example, we will demonstrate how this technique can be used to vary the Pickup animation based on the weight of the object.

Varying the pickup animation with a Blend Tree

Back in *Chapter 3, Interacting with the Environment*, we created character interaction with the environment by allowing the player character to pick up objects. A single animation sequence was used for this.

In the game, the character will need to pick up collectables of various sizes and weights. In order to visualize this variation in the game, we will be demonstrating a different use of Blend Trees.

In order to use a Blend Tree, a minimum of two motion clips is necessary. We supplemented the original pickup motion with another pickup animation to suit a heavier object.

Next, we will take a look at the differences between the two animation clips.

Viewing the pickup_heavy animation sequence

Once again, we will make use of the zombie_m character to preview the whole animation:

1. In the **Project** panel, click on the PACKT_Animations folder.

2. Locate the pickups asset.

3. Click on it to view its import settings in the **Inspector** panel.

The two animation clips contained in this FBX file have already been set up. The FBX file does not contain a model, so we will need another rigged model to preview the animation:

1. In the **Project** panel, click on the PACKT_Prefabs folder.

2. Drag the zombie_m prefab from the **Assets** panel into the animation preview panel at the bottom of the **Inspector** panel.

3. Take a look at the two motion clips to compare them:

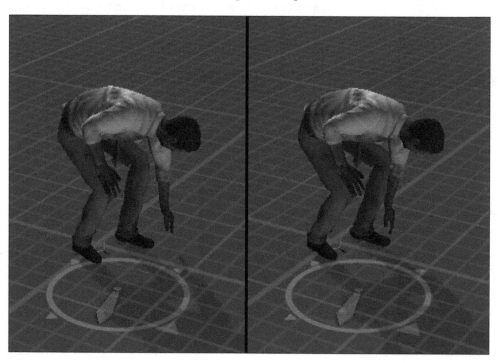

The illustration compares the contact point in both animation sequences. The left panel shows the original pickup animation and the right panel shows the heavier variation.

We can see some subtle differences in the pose, with the character's hips placed lower and feet spread further apart. In the context of the animation, this lower pose will convey more weight in the character's lift.

Note that the sequences are the same length.

Here we are only making minor changes that will blend together in the Blend Tree. If we wanted anything as extreme as a two-handed lift, it would be best to set this up in its own state.

The next stage will involve setting up the two animation sequences in a Blend Tree.

Creating a Blend Tree in the Pickup state

We will return to the animator controller to set up the Blend Tree for the pickup:

1. In the **Animator** window, right-click on the **Pickup** state and select **Create New Blend Tree** in **State**.

2. Double-click on the **Pickup** state to open the Blend Tree properties in the **Inspector** panel.

3. In the **Inspector** panel, rename the Blend Tree `Pickup_Blend_Tree`.

4. Click on the **+** symbol and select **Add Motion Field**.

5. Repeat this process to add a second motion field.

6. In the **Project** panel, navigate to the `PACKT_Animations` folder and locate the `Pickups` subfolder.

7. Click to expand `Pickups` and drag the pickup motion (indicated by the gray play button) into the first motion field in the **Inspector** panel.

8. Drag the `pickup_heavy` motion into the second motion field.

Now that we have added our motion clips, we can define the transition between them. We do this by first setting a parameter.

Setting the pickup Blend Tree parameter

Defining the blend requires a parameter which will tell the state machine when one motion sequence should stop and the other should start:

1. Locate the **Parameters** box in the lower-left of the **Animator** panel.
2. Click on the **+** symbol to create a new parameter.
3. Set the type to **Float**.
4. Rename the parameter `Weighting`.
5. Back in the **Inspector** panel, set the Blend Tree parameter to `Weighting`.

We are going to use the weight of the object (which will be contained in a variable) to determine the proportion of blend between the light pickup animation and the heavy pickup animation.

In theory, the value that is used to blend between the two clips can be anything we want, but we will do our best to use real-world values.

Unity uses **kilos** for its physics simulations, so we will try to stay consistent with this for our object weight values.

Let's assume that the original pickup animation will be used for anything up to 1 kilo (just over 2 pounds in imperial weight). This would cover light items such as food collectables and small amounts of ammunition.

When an object's weight exceeds 1 kilo, we start blending in the heavy pickup animation.

To allow the pickup Blend Tree to process this, we will set the blending threshold.

Setting the threshold for the pickup Blend Tree

We will continue adjusting the `Pickup_Blend_Tree` tree's parameters in the **Inspector** panel:

1. Uncheck the **Automate Thresholds** checkbox.
2. For the `pickup` clip, set the threshold to `1.0`.
3. Set the threshold for `pickup_heavy` to `4.0`.

These values will ensure that the original pickup animation is used for everything up to Weighting value of 1.0.

Once Weighting exceeds this value, the pickup_heavy clip is gradually blended in until it reaches a value of 4.0. At this point, it is purely the pickup_heavy animation which is being played:

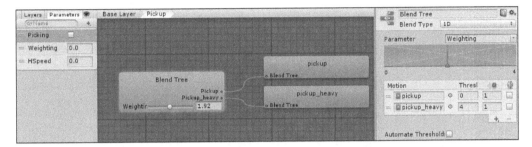

The next stage will involve storing the value of object in the character animation script.

Editing the character animation script to accommodate the pickup Blend Tree

Now that we have updated our animator controller, we will need to make a few changes to the character animation script to accommodate the additions:

1. In the **Project** panel, navigate to the PACKT_Scripts folder.

2. Click on it once, to view its contents in the **Assets** panel.

3. Locate FPSAnimation and double-click on it to open it in MonoDevelop.

4. At the top of the script, beneath the other variables add the following line of code:

```
var itemWeight : float;
```

As our blending parameter is a float, we set up the same kind of variable within the script. This will make transferring the values very simple.

Next, we will define the relationship between this variable and our animator controller.

5. Near the top of the `Pick` function, after the first statement, add the following code:

```
itemWeight = objectWeight;
thisAnimator.SetFloat("Weighting", objectWeight);
```

Here we tie together the animator parameter, `Weighting` with the script's variable `objectWeight`.

6. Save the script.

7. Minimize MonoDevelop.

At this point, if we test the game, the `pickup_heavy` animation will never be used, as there is nothing to tell the character animation script to set the `objectWeight` variable to a value higher than `1.0`.

Including this as a variable in the `collectable` script will make the value easy to adjust on individual collectable items.

Updating the Collectable script to include a weight variable

We will start where we left off in *Chapter 3, Interacting with the Environment*, with our `lunchBox` collectable prefab:

1. In the **Project** panel, click on the `PACKT_Prefabs` folder to view its contents in the **Assets** panel.

2. Locate the `lunchBox` prefab and drag it into the **Hierarchy** panel to instance it in the scene.

3. Use the **Move** tool to position the instanced `lunchBox` prefab somewhere in front of the player game object.

4. In the **Inspector** panel, click on the `Collectable` script, inside the **Collectable** component.

   The script will become highlighted in the **Assets** panel.

5. Double-click on the `Collectable` script in the **Assets** panel to open it in MonoDevelop.

6. Near the top of the script and after the other variables, add the following line of code:

```
var objectWeight = 0.25;
```

We create a float variable with the default value of 1.0 kilos (just over a half pound in imperial weight). This value seems realistic for this type of collectable.

As an exposed variable, the value of objectWeight will be visible and can be adjusted in the **Inspector** panel.

Our Collectable script does not yet pass its objectWeight value to the player animation script, so we will deal with that next.

Sending the objectWeight variable

The Collectable script already accesses the player animation script in order to tell it to set the **Picking Boolean** to true, which in turn causes the **Pickup** state to run.

All we have to do is have it send the objectWeight value to this script:

1. In MonoDevelop, make sure that the Collectable script is active in the editing window.
2. Scroll down until you can see all of the OnTriggerEnter function.
3. Locate the following statement:

   playerAnim.Pick();

4. Within the brackets, type the name of the variable that we have just added to the script.

The completed line of code should be:

playerAnim.Pick(objectWeight);

As the Collectable script already triggers the players Pick function, we have merely added the variable. Passing variables to functions in this way is often done when applying damage. Sending a weight value is much the same.

The last step is to modify the Pick statement inside the character animation script in order to recognize the variable that is being sent to it.

Updating the Pick function in the character animation script

In *Chapter 3, Interacting with the Environment*, we created the Pick function in the character animation script to enable the pickup animation to be played when the character comes in range of the collectable and presses a designated button.

Now that we included the `objectWeight` variable, we need to add this to the function to use the weight and blend the two motion clips accordingly:

1.   In MonoDevelop, select `FPSAnimation`.

2.   Scroll down until the `Pick` function is visible.

3.   Within the title brackets of the `Pick` function, add the following code:

     ```
     objectWeight : float
     ```

     The completed function should look like this:

     ```
     function Pick(objectWeight : float)
     {
         thisAnimator.SetTrigger("Picking");
     }
     ```

4.   Save the script.

Next, we will add a few more items to the scene so we can test the Blend Tree.

Testing the blended animation in the game

To check whether the blended animation works correctly, we will instance three different collectable items into our scene. We will use the `lunchBox` collectable that we worked with in *Chapter 3, Interacting with the Environment*, along with two heavier collectables—a first aid kit and a toolbox.

Instancing the collectable prefabs

The prefabs have already been set up, ready to be instanced in the game:

1.   Navigate to the `PACKT_Prefabs` folder and locate the `lunchBox`, `firstAidKit`, and `toolBox` prefabs.

2.   Create instances of all three prefabs by dragging them from the **Assets** panel into the **Hierarchy** panel.

3.   In the **Scene** view, move the collectable prefab objects so they are placed on the floor and located around 2 meters from each other. Arrange the objects in the order of weight, with the `lunchBox` collectible first, then `firstAidKit`, and lastly `toolBox`.

     We need to hook up the variables.

4.   Select all three collectables in the **Hierarchy** panel.

5. Drag the `player_m` game object from the **Hierarchy** panel into the **Player Obj** slot in the **Inspector** panel.

6. Drag the `FirstPersonCharacter` game object into the **Player Camera** slot.

7. Expand the `FPSController` game object's hierarchy if necessary and drag the `zombie_m_Head` game object into the **Head Bone** slot.

8. Select the `firstAidBox` game object and set its `Object Weight` variable to `2.5` in the **Inspector** panel.

9. Select the `toolBox` game object and set its `Object Weight` to `4`.

The collectable prefabs each have a trigger and a variable assigned for the weight, which will be interpreted by the character animation script that we just edited:

Now that we have set up the Blend Tree, character animation script, and added the collectable prefabs to the game, we can preview the animation.

Previewing the blended animation

To make sure that our Blend Tree is working correctly, we will need to view the animator panel when we are previewing the game:

1. Drag the **Animator** tab to the space beside the **Game** view panel and scale it so that the Blend Tree is clearly visible.

2. Press the **Play** button in the top-center of the Unity interface.

3. Using the *W, A, S, D,* or cursor keys, move the player to the first of the three instanced prefabs.

4. When he has picked up the `lunchBox` collectible, move on to the next collectable.

Watch the animation in the game view, there should be a noticeable variation in the character's movement to suggest a difference in the weight of the objects.

This variation should also be evident in the Blend Tree display in the **Animator** panel.

When the player character is picking up the `lunchBox` collectible, the `pickup_light` blend field is active. When picking up the `toolBox` collectible, the `pickup_heavy` blend field is active, and when picking up `firstAidKit`, the Blend Tree mixes between the two blend fields:

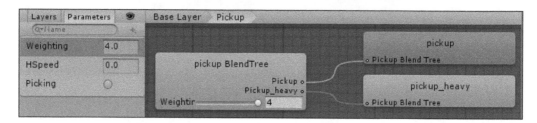

Summary

In this chapter, we introduced the Blend Tree as a method of blending similar animations to create more realistic animated responses during the game.

Our exercises demonstrated two different implementations of this:

In the first example, we added strafe animations to the `Idle` state to give the player feedback when moving from side to side.

In the second implementation, we created variation in the pickup animation by blending light and heavy variations of the motion sequence based on the determined weight of the object that was picked up.

In the next chapter, we will return to the enemies to demonstrate **ragdoll** effects.

As a physics effect, the ragdoll prefab is commonly used to simulate the physical properties of weight and force resulting in more convincing death sequences for player and non-player character objects.

Although these physics effects do not use the Mecanim toolset, they will complement our state machine by adding further realism to our enemy and environment in the game.

8
Implementing Ragdoll Physics

In this chapter, we will apply physics to the female zombie character, creating an interesting death effect that can be used in the game.

Ragdoll physics is a method that involves a system of joints connecting weighted body parts used to create a real-time animation sequence.

Unlike, traditional keyframe animation that is created in external 3D software and imported to Unity, the ragdoll object will interact with forces within the game. This means that the enemy will fall to the ground in different ways based on the applied force and the scenery that it collides with.

In this chapter, you will learn to:

- Demonstrate the use of Unity's Rigidbody and Joint components
- Demonstrate the creation of a ragdoll from an existing character with the Ragdoll Wizard
- Show the adjustment of collision objects to fit the character model
- Add custom joints for parts of the rig not covered by the wizard
- Set limits to approximate realistic joint rotation.

When the zombie character is killed, we will replace the animated game object with the ragdoll game object, allowing it to fall to the ground and react with other physical objects.

We will start with a brief overview of Unity's joints.

Introduction to joints in Unity

Creating a ragdoll game object in Unity requires some basic knowledge of the different joints and how these can be added to game objects.

Unlike the joints or bones that are imported in the FBX file as part of the rigged model, Unity's joints can be used to connect game objects that respond to physics within the game.

There are several different joints that we can choose from, which suit different situations within a game, and different joints in a human body.

Creating a test scene

We will start with a blank scene and some simple geometry to test our physics objects:

1. Create a new scene by navigating to **File | New Scene....**
2. Add a plane game object using the menu bar by navigating to **GameObject | 3D Object | Plane**.
3. Click on the **Plane** in the **Scene** view or **Project** panel to adjust its parameters in the **Inspector** panel.

    The plane game object should be centered within the scene by default.

4. Rename the plane `groundPlane` by typing this into the field at the top of the **Inspector** panel.
5. In the **Transform Scale** fields, set the position **X** and **Z** values both to `0.25`.

    This will make the plane large enough that it will catch the ragdoll as it falls, allowing us to test the effect as it hits the ground.

    Next, we will create two more game objects with which we will test the joints.

6. Create a sphere game object from the menu bar by navigating to **GameObject | 3D Object | Sphere**.
7. Select the object to access its parameters in the **Inspector** panel.
8. Set its **Transform Scale** values to `0.5`.
9. Create a cube game object by navigating to **GameObject | 3D Object | Cube**.

10. In the **Inspector** panel, set its **Transform Scale** values to 0.5.

11. Position the cube and sphere close together somewhere above the groundPlane object:

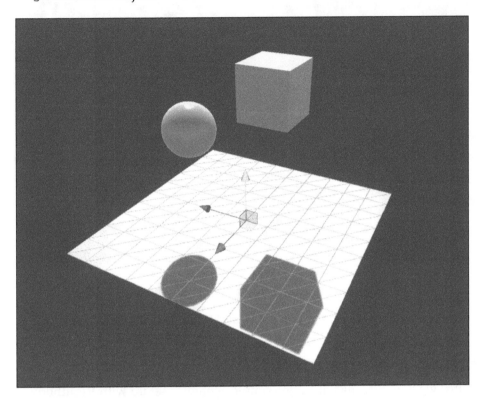

Our test objects will have colliders as components by default, but we will need to add a **Rigidbody** component to the sphere and cube to allow them to respond to physics.

12. From the menu bar, add a **Rigidbody** component to the cube by navigating to **Components | Physics | Rigidbody**.

13. Add a **Rigidbody** component to the sphere.

    By default the rigidbodies' **Use Gravity** parameter will be checked, enabling it, and **Mass** will be set to 1.

14. Point the default scene camera at the group of objects, so we can see them in the **Game** view.

15. Test the game by pressing the **Play** button.

The two objects should fall onto `groundPlane`:

Our next step will involve connecting the sphere and cube with a joint.

The objects are not connected at this point, and will fall at the same rate.

Adding a hinge joint

Now that we have a scene with some simple geometry set up with **Rigidbody** components, we can test one of Unity's joints to see what it can do:

1. Select the sphere.

2. Add a **Hinge Joint** component from the menu bar by navigating to **Components | Physics | Hinge Joint**.

   The component's parameters will become visible in the **Inspector** panel.

   The **Hinge Joint** component's first parameter, **Connected Body**, has a field where we can drag another object.

3. Drag the **Cube** game object from the **Hierarchy** panel into the **Connected Body** field in the **Inspector** panel.

4. Set the **Anchor** and **Axis** values in the **X** field to 1.

5. Set the **Anchor** and **Axis** values in the **Y** and **Z** fields to 0.

6. Uncheck the **Auto Configure Connected** checkbox.

7. Enter the value 2.5 for **X** in the **Connected Anchor** field.

8. Zero out the other **Y** and **Z** for **Connected Anchor** fields.

9. Check the **Use Spring** checkbox.

10. Set the **Spring** value to 0.4 and the **Damper** value to 0.25.

 Spring effects are not always used in ragdoll simulations, but adding it here will help us to exaggerate the function of the hinge.

The resulting **Hinge Joint** component should match the illustration here:

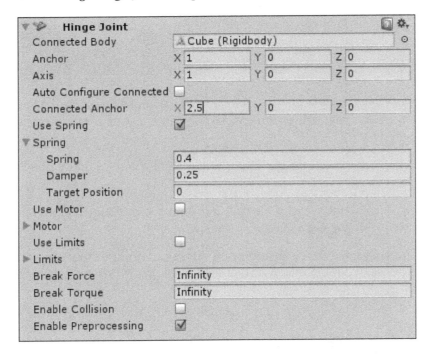

In order to properly test the hinge, we will need to ensure that the objects are weighted differently.

11. Select the cube and under its **Rigidbody** component, change the **Mass** value to 5.

12. Test the game by pressing the **Play** button:

At this point, the cube and sphere will fall at different rates, because they are connected with the hinge joint the heavier cube will appear to drag the sphere with it.

When it contacts the `groundPlane` object, sphere will bounce slightly due to the spring.

Now that we have demonstrated the basics of joint components in Unity, we can move on to creating the ragdoll.

It would be tedious and time consuming to set up each joint connecting each of the character's bones, but luckily Unity has a tool, the Ragdoll Wizard, which automates the process.

Creating the ragdoll object

We will create the ragdoll prefab using our female zombie character. We need to make a few changes to the scene before we add the character model:

1. Delete the `Sphere` and `Cube` objects.

2. In the **Hierarchy** panel, select the `groundPlane` game object.

3. In **the Inspector panel**, set the `groundPlane` object's **Transform Scale** field's **X** and **Z** values to `0.5`.

4. In the **Project** panel, click on the `FBX_Imports` folder to view its contents in the **Assets** panel.

5. In the **Assets** panel, locate `zombie_f` and drag it into the **Hierarchy** panel, instancing it in your scene.

> In previous chapters, we have already created an enemy character prefab from this model, but for the ragdoll prefab we do not need the character controller, animator controller, or behavior script, so it saves time to just create the ragdoll from the source model.

The female zombie model will load in the scene with the default material. We can add the correct material next.

Assigning the material

Adding the right material will make it easier for us to notice any stretching on the surface of the mesh and correct the joint limits:

1. In the **Project** panel, click on the `PACKT_Materials` folder to view its contents in the **Assets** panel.

2. In the **Assets** panel, locate `zombie_f` and drag it onto the character model in the **Scene** view:

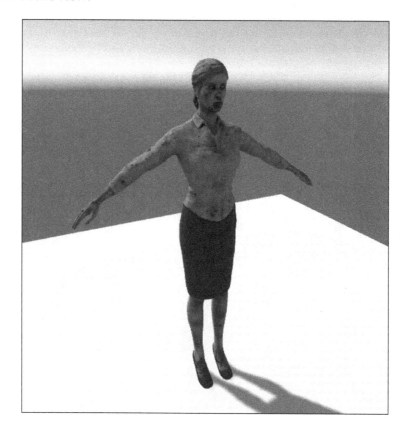

The correct material will appear on the model.

Generating the initial ragdoll

The **Ragdoll Wizard** is a tool within Unity designed to create a basic ragdoll from a jointed and skinned character model. It works by creating a relationship between each of the major bones in the skeleton:

1. In the **Hierarchy** panel, select the `zombie_f` game object.

2. From the menu bar, navigate to **GameObject | 3D Object | Ragdoll**.

The **Create Ragdoll** window will appear in the interface prompting you to assign the bones to the ragdoll hierarchy.

Assigning bones to the ragdoll list

The **Create Ragdoll** window consists of a number of fields in which we must specify the hierarchy of the character model by dragging bones into the appropriate slots:

1. In the **Hierarchy** panel, *Alt* + click the small arrow next to `zombie_f` to fully expand its hierarchy.

2. Drag `zombie_f_Pelvis` onto the **Pelvis** slot in the **Create Ragdoll** window.

3. Drag the appropriate bones into the fields in the **Create Ragdoll** window:

    ◦ For the hips fields, use the thigh bones

    ◦ For the knee fields, use calf bones

    ◦ For the **Middle Spine** field, use spine2

    ◦ Complete the list by dragging the rest of the bones to fill the positions in the window

Note that not all bones in the hierarchy have their own fields in the list—just the major joints that are expected to articulate during the ragdoll animation.

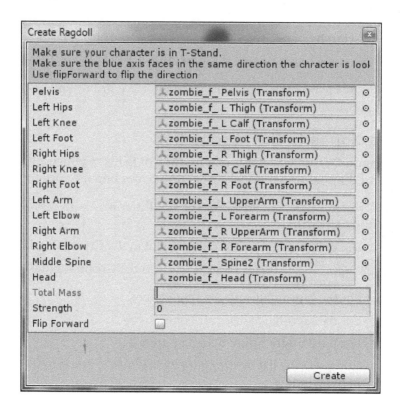

When all the fields are full, the warning message at the bottom of the window will disappear.

Assigning mass

For the different bones in the ragdoll to fall and collide realistically, we need to assign mass. Unity will then calculate the mass of each individual bone and assign these values to the appropriate **Rigidbody** component:

1. In the field for **Total Mass**, enter 52. This is the weight in kilos of the character.

2. Leave **Strength** at its default setting of 0 and the **Flip Forward** checkbox unchecked.

    We will be applying force in our script.

    The **Create** button at the bottom of the window should now be active.

3. Click on the **Create** button to set up the ragdoll.

An arrangement of collision objects and gizmos will be added to the character game object:

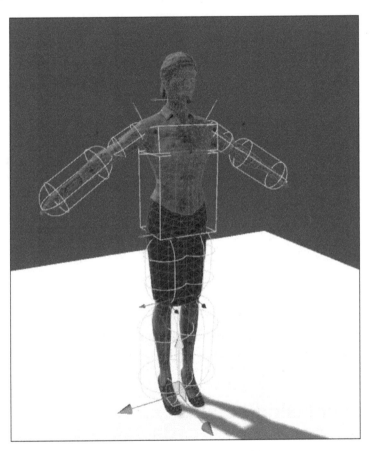

Previewing the default ragdoll

The character now has a series of collision objects, rigidbodies, and joints added to its bones. We can now see the ragdoll functioning. To preview the ragdoll click on the **Play** button in the top center of the Unity interface.

The character should drop to the ground:

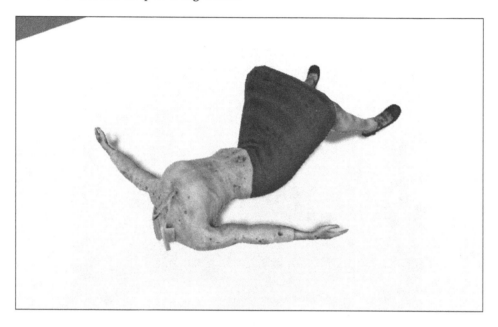

The result is not exactly what we want, but this is actually a good start. We can get better results with a few adjustments.

Each collision object has a default size and each joint has its own default rotation limits, which have been set up to approximate the normal rotation of human joints. In the next step, we will adjust these.

Adjusting collision objects

In video games, collision objects are usually simple objects, which are used to approximate the physical boundaries of more complex forms.

In the humanoid figure, these take the form of boxes, cylinders, and spheres.

When the ragdoll is switched on (by pressing the **Play** to run the game), gravity is applied to the character and each connected joint will drop down until its own collision object hits another.

From looking at the results, we can see that there are some problems:

- Firstly, the leg joints get stuck leaving the character arched over with her legs still placed on the ground
- Secondly, the head intersects with the ground

We will take a closer look at the collision object settings to solve these problems.

Adjusting the radius of the capsule collider to fit the leg

When the ragdoll is created, Unity assigns collision objects to different joints to approximate their physical volume. Often the default settings for each collider need to be adjusted to ensure that this volume is correct for the part of the character model that it is applied to.

1. In the **Hierarchy** panel, select the `zombie_f_L_Thigh` object.

   The object's parameters will become visible in the **Inspector** panel. Its components are a **Rigidbody**, **Character Joint**, and **Capsule Collider**.

   We will adjust the capsule collider's parameters in the next step.

2. In the **Inspector** panel, scroll down until you can see the **Capsule Collider** properties.

3. Decrease the **Radius** until the capsule is the same size as the widest part of the character's thigh. A setting of `3.09` should be pretty close.

Leave the remaining properties at their default settings:

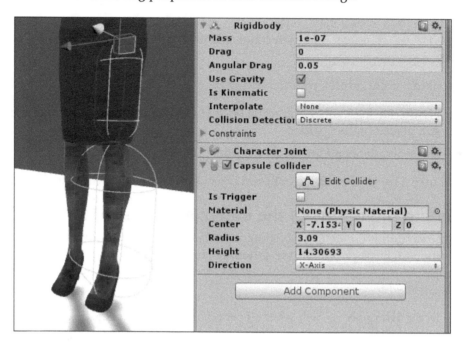

4. Repeat this process for the right thigh.

5. Change the **Radius** value of the **Capsule Collider** attached to each of the calves to 2.29.

   The objective is to make the collision objects match the size of the body part as close as possible, ensuring that this part of the character model does not appear to float above or intersect with the ground or any other object.

6. Preview the ragdoll a second time.

The results should show a big improvement—the character will drop all the way to the ground and the legs will collapse naturalistically.

Our next step is to fix the head.

Adjusting the head's collider

By default, the head will have a sphere collider component to define its volume. With the default settings, the sphere collider's small size is causing the head to intersect with the ground plane.

In this step, we will adjust the collider to fit the character's head:

1. In the **Hierarchy** panel, click on `zombie_f_Head`.

   In the **Inspector** panel, we can see that the head has **Rigidbody**, **Character Joint**, and **Sphere Collider** components.

   By default, the **Radius** value of the sphere collider is too low for it to adequately collide with the ground object. It is also positioned too low and far back to completely surround the skull.

2. In the **Inspector** panel, rescale the sphere collider's **Radius** to around `3.26`.

3. Align the collider within the head by adjusting the **Center** values in the **X** and **Y** fields until the collider fits just around the head in the side view.

4. The **Center Z** value actually controls the horizontal position of the collider, so this can be left at `0`.

   The sphere collider will not be a perfect fit because the head is not round, but try to fit the top half of the head as this part will most likely be colliding with other objects in the game.

> If you are working with a model that has a particularly long head, you can also replace the sphere with a capsule collider such as those used in the limbs.

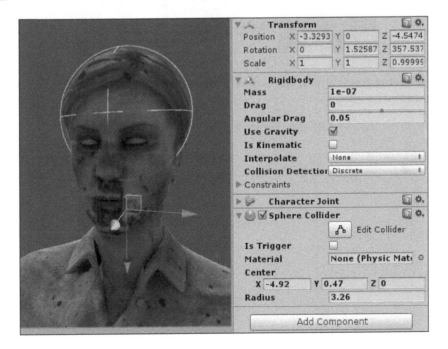

We need to scale down the box collider attached to the Spine2 object so that the arms can fall more closely to the torso.

5. In the **Hierarchy** panel, select zombie_f_Spine2.

6. Change the scale and position of the box to better approximate the hard, bony areas of the torso:

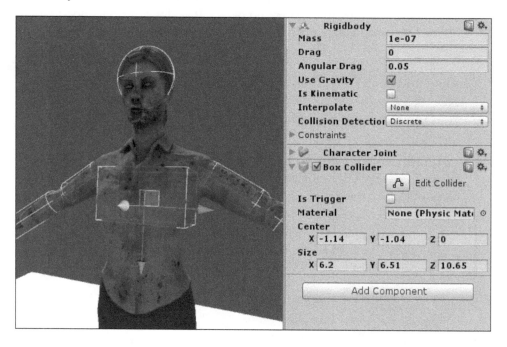

Reducing the width of the box will allow the arms to fall across the body more naturally.

7. Preview the ragdoll once more, by clicking on the **Play** button.

The results should show improvement, but there are some issues with the arms of the character intersecting with the torso when the zombie falls to the ground.

This problem is not just due to the scale of the colliders but rather the rotational limits of the character joints, which we will adjust next:

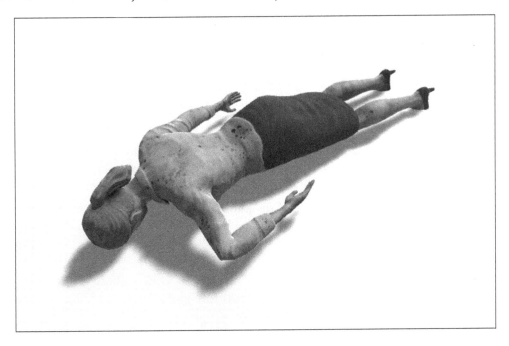

Fine-tuning the character joints

Character joints are fully adjustable joints that can be adjusted to suit various situations. They can be set up to limit the range of motion on all three axes.

Rotational limits were applied to all of the joints when the ragdoll object was created. We will need to adjust these settings in order to correct the range of rotation for the arm.

Adjusting the rotational limits of the upper arm

Limiting the range of movement in the arm joints will help us prevent the arms intersecting with the torso when the character drops to the ground:

1. In the **Hierarchy** panel, select `zombie_f_R_UpperArm`.

2. The game object's components and their values will become visible in the **Inspector** panel.

   We can begin to adjust the settings of the character joint starting at the top of the list of properties.

3. **Connected Body** is the parent object that the joint (in this case the right arm) is connected to. The object must have a **Rigidbody** component attached in order to complete the chain of bones and for the ragdoll to function correctly.

4. **Anchor** is the point of origin of the joint. Values of `0, 0, 0` inherit the exact position of the joint's game object parent—in this case, the `zombie_f_Spine2` bone, to which the joint is attached. Change the value in the **X** field to `-1.5`, moving the anchor further from the center of the character.

5. **Axis** allows you to set the direction in which the joint is allowed to twist. Basically, an offset from the orientation of the parent object. By default, the joint is set up to twist negatively on the **Z** axis.

6. **Swing Axis** allows you to set the direction which the joint is allowed to rotate. By default, the joint is set up to swing negatively on the **Y** axis.

7. **Low Twist Limit** is the value in degrees that the joint can twist negatively on the specified axis. By default, this is set to `-70`. Change this to `-50`.

8. **High Twist Limit** is the value in degrees that the joint can twist positively on the specified axis. By default, set to `10`. Change this to `40`.

9. **Swing 1 Limit** is the value in degrees that the joint can swing negatively on the specified axis. By default, set to `50`. Change this to `70`.

10. **Swing 2 Limit** is the value in degrees that the joint can swing positively on the specified axis. By default, set to `0`. Change this to `50`.

11. **Break Force** is the amount of force that needs to be applied in order to break the joint, separating the two bones.

12. **Break Torque** is the amount of torque that needs to be applied in order to break the joint.

These last two properties are set to Infinity by default ensuring that no amount of force will separate the joints.

Before moving on to the lower arm joint:

1. Scale down the **Radius** of the **Capsule Collider** component in the zombie_f_R_UpperArm object. A radius of 1.45 should work well.

2. Adjust the left-upper arm with similar settings to definite its limits and collider size.

Adjusting the rotational limits of the forearm

We will carry on and adjust the forearm joint to complete the right arm.

1. In the **Hierarchy** panel, select zombie_f_R_Forearm. Its properties will become visible in the **Inspector** panel.

2. In the **Character Joint** component, expand and look at the settings for **Axis**, **Swing Axis**, and all **Limits**:

   ◦ The **Axis** is set up to twist the joint negatively on the **Y** axis.

   ◦ The **Swing Axis** is set up to swing on the **Z** axis. This will rotate the forearm forward.

   ◦ The **Low Twist Limit** has been set to -90, which twists the elbow. Decrease this to 0.

   ◦ The **High Twist Limit** has been set by default to 0, which is appropriate for an elbow joint which only rotates in one direction.

   ◦ Set the **Swing 1 Limit** value to 30 to allow the forearm to swing backwards slightly.

   ◦ Set the **Swing 2 Limit** value to 100 to allow the forearm to swing forward.

   We can leave the remaining **Character Joint** settings with their default values.

3. In the **Inspector** panel, scale down the capsule collider's **Radius** to an appropriate value. A setting of 1.6 should ensure that it tightly fits around the forearm.

4. Repeat these adjustments to the **Character Joints** and **Capsule Colliders** of the left arm before moving on to the head.

Adjusting the rotational limits of the head

Earlier in this chapter, we adjusted the **Radius** and **Center** fields of the head's sphere collider to better approximate the proportions of the character mesh.

Now, we need to adjust its rotational limits in the head's character joint:

1. In the **Hierarchy** panel, select zombie_f_Head. Its parameters and components will become visible in the **Inspector** panel.

    For the head, the **Axis** value represents the forward and back movement of the head.

2. The **Swing Axis** value represents the side-to-side movement. Set the **Swing1 Limit** to 40.

Previewing the adjusted ragdoll

Press the **Play** button again to view the result of the adjustments we made to the character joints and colliders:

Once again, the results of the ragdoll have been improved, but now that we adjusted the components in the head, it becomes obvious that the ponytail is pointing upward, not hanging down toward the ground as we would expect it to.

When we initially ran the Ragdoll Wizard, there were no joints assigned to the ponytail. We will fix this by adding our own character joint to this part of the character.

Adding a custom joint to the ragdoll

Any bone can have a character joint attached to it and be added to the ragdoll animation, but it is important to respect the hierarchy of joints. In this case, it means maintaining the connection between the ponytail and the head.

After following through the previous sections in this chapter, you may have noticed that a body part requires three components to be included in a ragdoll: **Collider**, **Rigidbody**, and **Joint**.

We will add these one at a time and adjust the settings to make the ponytail react in a realistic way.

Adding a capsule collider to the ponytail

Next, we will add the necessary components to make the ponytail work with our ragdoll:

1. In the **Hierarchy** panel, select `zombie_f_Ponytail1`.

2. From the menu bar, navigate to **Component | Physics | Capsule Collider** to add the collider component to the selected game object.

   For organic or cylindrical organic forms, the capsule collider is a good choice because it has a rounded cross-section and a rounded end. This type of collider has already been used in the arms and legs of the character ragdoll.

3. In the **Inspector** panel, set the value in the **Center X** field to `-0.91`, **Y** to `-2.63`, and leave **Z** at its default `0`.

4. Increase the radius to `1.03`.

5. Increase the height to 6.58.

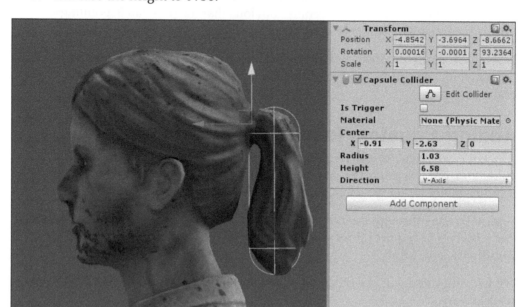

The new capsule collider should fit neatly around the character's ponytail.

Adding a Rigidbody component

The capsule collider defines the physical volume of the ponytail, but we need to add a **Rigidbody** component for it to respond to physics:

1. From the menu bar, navigate to **Component | Physics | Rigidbody**.

   When we initially created the ragdoll, we specified **Total Mass** of 52 kilos for the whole character. The Ragdoll Wizard divided up this weight proportionately among the various rigidbodies attached to the bones.

   Here, we must manually add a mass for the ponytail.

2. In **Inspector**, enter the value 0.125 in the **Mass** field of the ponytail1 object's **Rigidbody** component.

3. Leave the remaining properties at their default values.

Adding the character joint

At this point, the ponytail will be affected by physics in our Unity scene, but it needs to be properly connected to the head using a **Joint** component:

1. From the menu bar, navigate to **Component | Physics | Character Joint**.

2. In the **Hierarchy** panel, drag zombie_f_Head onto the **Connected Body** field in the **Inspector** panel.

    This will ensure that the ponytail follows the rotation of the head.

3. In the **Anchor** group, decrease the **X** value to -0.48 and increase the **Y** value to 0.08. Leave **Z** at its default 0.

4. Leave the remaining settings at their default values.

When the animation is previewed, the ponytail will now respond to fall and collide along with the other jointed body parts:

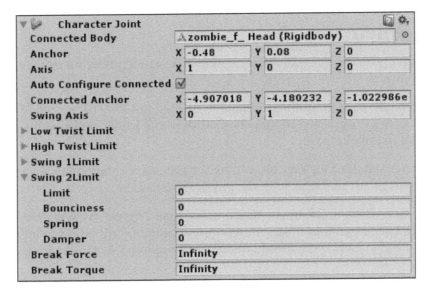

Unity's Ragdoll Wizard is a very fast way to set up a basic humanoid ragdoll, but when we need to accommodate extra character features such as a ponytail, large nose, or an extra limb, the necessary components can be quickly added to really make the ragdoll fit the character model.

Saving the ragdoll as a prefab

To be able to instantiate the ragdoll during our game with a script it needs to be saved as a prefab:

1. In the **Hierarchy** panel, select the `zombie_f` game object.

2. In the **Inspector** panel, rename the game object `zombie_f _ragdoll`.

3. Select and delete the animator component.

4. In the **Project** panel, click on the `PACKT_Prefabs` folder to view its contents in the **Assets** panel.

5. Drag the game object into an empty area of the **Assets** panel to create the prefab.

In the **Hierarchy** panel, the game object will turn blue, indicating that it is an instance of a prefab. We can instantiate the ragdoll in a number of scenes.

Summary

In this chapter, we demonstrated the creation of a ragdoll proxy for our female zombie character.

Starting with the default settings initiated in the Ragdoll Wizard, we made small adjustments to the physics components: **Colliders** and **Joints**, tailoring the ragdoll rig to better fit our character.

Finally, we customized the ragdoll, adding the necessary components to incorporate a unique part of our character with the physics simulation.

In *Chapter 9, Controlling Enemy Animation with AI and Triggers*, we will demonstrate the finalized enemy character scripts, which will explain scripted behavior and character state, including the instantiation of our ragdoll object in the game.

9

Controlling Enemy Animation with AI and Triggers

In the last chapter, we looked at using ragdoll physics to add some realistic effects to our enemy death sequence.

In this chapter, we will build on the enemy AI that we began in *Chapter 6, Talking Heads*, creating three different behaviors for the enemy character within the game.

We will tackle the following aspects of the enemy AI:

- Targeting the player with range detection
- Making the enemy patrol
- Controlling root movement curves
- Attacking the player
- Injuring the enemy and implementing the ragdoll effect
- Obstacle detection and reaction
- Implementing pathfinding with navMesh

Implementing range detection

Our work in *Chapter 6, Talking Heads*, left us with an enemy that becomes aware of the player on a button click. Let's begin where we left off and improve this to make a smarter enemy that automatically attacks the player when he comes within a certain range.

Looking at the scene

We will start by opening our scene:

1. In the Unity project, open `Chapter9_Start` by navigating to **File | Open Scene... | Chapter9_Start**.

    The scene consists of the main office geometry and a single female zombie character. The `FPSController` prefab will allow us to navigate the scene.

2. Press the **Play** button in the top center of the Unity interface.

The female zombie is currently set up to idle in place. We can approach and nothing happens at this point:

In the next step, we will add the zombie's AI script and allow her to detect the player.

Adding the initial AI script

We are starting with the zombie's script that we completed in *Chapter 6, Talking Heads*. The enemy is able to target the player, but we need to add some more code for anything exciting to happen:

1. In the **Project** panel, locate the PACKT_Scripts folder.

2. Click on it to view its contents it in the **Assets** panel.

3. Locate zombie_chapter9_Start.

4. Drag the script onto the zombie_f game object in the **Inspector** panel.

   We now need to hook up some variables.

5. Drag the FPSController game object from the **Hierarchy** panel onto the **Target** slot under the **zombie_Chapter9 (script)** component in the **Inspector** panel.

   This will allow the zombie to find the player.

6. In the **Project** panel, locate PACKT_Sounds and click on it once to view its contents in the **Inspector** panel.

7. Drag zombie_growl onto the **Snarl Sound** slot in the **Inspector** panel.

This will allow us to hear the zombie's growl when she is alerted.

If we preview the game at this point, we will have the same kind of setup as the end of *Chapter 6, Talking Heads*. The zombie will not notice the player until the fire button is pressed. In the next section, we will make the zombie respond to the player getting close.

Adding proximity detection to the enemy AI script

The zombie currently becomes aware of the player only when the fire button is pressed. We need to add the necessary code for the zombie to detect the player:

1. In the **Project** panel, locate the PACKT_Scripts folder and click on it to view its contents in the **Assets** panel.

2. Locate zombie_chapter9_Start in the **Assets** panel.

3. Double-click on the script to open it in MonoDevelop.

   We will start by adding some variables.

4. Add the following line of code to the end of the list of variables at the top of the script:

```
var distance : float;
var awareRange : float = 4.0;
```

   The first variable that we add is a `float` variable that will be used to store the current distance between the zombie and her target. The second, also a `float` variable that defines the range within which the zombie will become aware of the player.

5. In the `Update` function, locate the following code:

```
if(Input.GetButton("Fire1") && alerted == false)
{
    alerted = true;
}
```

6. Replace it with the following:

```
distance = Vector3.Distance(target.position,
transform.position);
if(distance <= awareRange)
{
    alerted = true;
}
```

   The `distance` variable keeps track of the actual distance between the zombie and the target using the `Vector3.Distance` method.

   In the `if` statement, we check to see if distance is less than the `awareRange` value, which we defined at the top of the script as a value of `4.0`. When this is the case we set the `alerted` boolean to true.

7. Save the behavior script and test the game by pressing the **Play** button.

The zombie will idle for a while before walking forward. Once she comes within 4 meters of the player, she will become alerted to the player's presence and walk toward him:

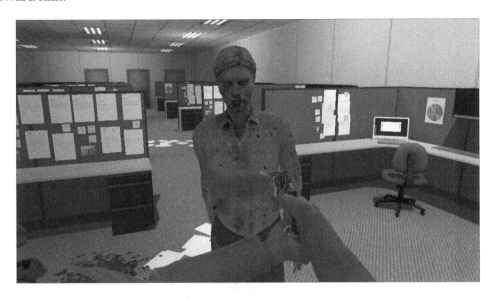

This small addition to the script makes for a slightly more intelligent AI, but it has limited uses in the game.

The current animator controller contains three states: **Idle**, **Turn**, and **Walk**. The script switches between these states by setting triggers in the controller.

In the next section, we will set up a patrol behavior for the enemy, so the player can use good timing to avoid being detected.

Setting up the patrol behavior

We already have a zombie that will move toward the player when he comes within range, but a room full of zombies doing the same thing will not make the game particularly fun.

When our player has run out of bullets, we still want to give them the opportunity to survive the game using stealth. We can do this by giving enemies fixed patrol patterns, which the player must identify in order to bide his time and sneak through the level.

Adding variables for the patrol

We will prepare the script by defining a few more variables to our current enemy script:

1. Open or maximize MonoDevelop and make sure that the `zombie_Chapter9_Start` script is active in the editing window.

2. Add the following code to the bottom of the list of variables near the top of the script:

```
var patrolPts : Transform[];
var currPt : int;
var targetedPt : Transform;
var ptDistance : float;
var changeDistance : float = 0.5;
var turnTime : float = 5.0;
var moving : boolean = true;
var speed : float;
var alertDistance : float = 3.0;
```

Here, we are defining `patrolPts` as an array of transforms. This will store the positions of a number of patrol points (or waypoints) in the game level.

The next variable, `currPt` will keep track of which `patrolPt` the zombie is currently targeting. Next, `targetedPt` maintains a connection to the current point's transform.

The `ptDistance` float variable will keep track of how far the zombie is from the targeted point.

The next variable, `changeDistance` will define the distance which causes the zombie to target the next point, here we are defining it with the value `0.5`.

We added `turnTime` temporarily to determine how long it will take the zombie to turn to face the next point.

After this, we have a boolean named `moving` that will let us determine when the zombie should be moving forward.

We already have a float parameter to determine the zombie's `walkSpeed`, but we add a float named `speed` to keep track of the current value and help us decide which animation to play.

Finally, `alertDistance` will determine when the zombie can see the player.

Adding the initial patrol code to the Update function

We will use the variables that we just added in the next lines of code:

1. Near the top of the `Update` function, add the following code:

    ```
    targetedPt = patrolPts[currPt];
    var patrolPtDistance : float =
    Vector3.Distance(targetedPt.position, transform.position);
    var playerDistance = Vector3.Distance(target.position,
    transform.position);

    if(playerDistance <= alertDistance)
    {
        alerted = true;
    }
    ```

    Here, we define the `targetedPt` variable as the transform current in the `patrolPt` array.

    We define a new local float variable named `patrolPtDistance`, which keeps track of the distance between the `targetedPt` variable's position and the game object's position.

    Variables that are only used within a single function can be kept as local variables like this to reduce clutter in the **Inspector** panel.

    Another local variable, `playerDistance`, uses the same method, `Vector3.Distance` to keep track of the distance between the player and the enemy. This one will be used to tell the zombie when to leave her idling routine and go into attack mode.

    Following this variable definition, we add an `if` statement to check whether `playerDistance` is less than or equal to `alertDistance`. When this is the case, we switch the `alerted` boolean to `true`.

    We are prioritizing functionality here, the zombie's reaction to the player is more important than the patrol.

2. Locate the `if(alerted)` statement and add the following line of code at the start:

    ```
    targetedPt = target;
    ```

    This will override our patrol point targeting and allow the zombie to chase after the player rather than the point.

The next line of code in the script calls the function `TurnToPlayer`. We will repurpose this function to also turn the zombie toward the current patrol point.

3. Replace `TurnToPlayer()` with `TurnToPoint()`.

4. Right after the closing bracket of the `if(alerted)` statement, further down in the `Update` function, enter the following code:

```
else
{
    if(patrolPtDistance <= changeDistance)
    {
        ChangePt();
        turning = true;
    }
}
```

Here, we check to see if the zombie has come within range of the patrol point. We want her to start her turn a little way before she gets to the actual point.

We run a new custom function called `ChangePt`, which will update the patrol point in the array so the zombie has something to turn toward.

5. Add the following code right after the last statement:

```
if(turning)
{
    TurnToPoint();

    if(angle < 2 && angle > -2)
    {
        WalkTowards();
    }
}
```

Here we check for the boolean `turning` to be true, which is also set up to run the **Turn** state in our animator controller.

If the current angle that we need to turn to face toward the patrol point is less than 2 degrees difference in the positive or negative direction, we run the `WalkTowards` function which we have already defined.

6. After the `Update` function add the following code:

```
function ChangePt()
{
    currPt++;
}
```

This is a very short function. All we are doing here is increasing the `currPt` variable, which will move on to the next patrol point in the array. This code needs to be outside the `Update` function, otherwise the number will continuously increase when `turning` is `true`.

If we play the game at this point, we will very quickly get an *index out of range* error. The `currPt` variable will increase way beyond the number of items we have in our array, so we need to limit it.

7. To fix this, we will add the following code to the very end of the `Update` function:

```
if(currPt > patrolPts.Length-1)
{
    currPt = 0;
}
```

Here, we are ensuring that whenever `currPt` is greater than the length of the `patrolPts` array (`-1`, because we count from 0), `currPt` is equal to `0`.

The value of `CurrPt` will never be greater than the number of items we have in our array.

We now run the `TurnToPoint` function in two situations in our script, but the point that we turn to is `target`, which will be set up to use the player's transform. We need to edit this function to use our new variable.

8. Locate the `TurnToPlayer` function and rename it `TurnToPoint`.

9. Within the function, replace the second line of code with the following:

```
var localRotate =
transform.InverseTransformPoint(targetedPt.position);
```

All we need to do here is replace the variable `target` with the new `targetedPt` variable, which is set to the player or the current patrol point in the main part of our script.

We created the `WalkTowards` function back in *Chapter 6, Talking Heads*. It basically allows the zombie to move forward on her local axis while running the walk animation.

We should ensure that the zombie is not turning when this happens.

10. Locate the `WalkTowards` function and add the following code right at the top:

```
turning = false;
```

11. Save the script.

In order to see if this code works, we need to set up some patrol points for the zombie to use in the level. We will do this next.

Defining patrol points

We will start by creating two patrol points (or waypoints) in the scene, though the script that we created will accept more than this.

The script defines the patrol points as **Transforms**. We could use empty game objects or pretty much anything we want.

We will use cubes here, because you can see them clearly in the scene. We can delete the mesh renderers or just turn them off before we build the game so that we do not see them:

1. Create a `cube` game object using the menu bar by navigating to **Game Object | 3D Object | Cube**.

2. At the top of the **Inspector** panel, change the name of the game object to `wayPoint01`.

3. Decrease the **Transform - Scale** values for **X**, **Y**, and **Z** to `0.5`.

4. Deactivate the **Box Collider** component by unchecking the box next to this component's name.

5. Duplicate the waypoint by selecting it and using the *Ctrl + D* shortcut (*Cmd + D* on a Mac).

6. In **Inspector** panel, rename the second box `wayPoint02`.

7. In the scene, position `wayPoint01` so that it is between the first set of office cube partitions and `wayPoint02` so that it is between the third set.

8. Move both waypoints so that they are resting on the ground.

   You can set the **Position Y** value to `0.25` in the **Transform** settings at the top of the **Inspector** panel if you want to be exact.

9. If necessary, reposition the `zombie_f` game object so that the zombie is facing toward `wayPoint01`, with her back to `wayPoint02` a short distance away:

Now that we have all of our game objects repositioned, we can add the two waypoints to the array in the behavior script.

10. Select the `zombie_f` game object in the **Hierarchy** panel.

    The script component should now be visible in the **Inspector** panel.

11. In the **Inspector** panel, click on the small arrow next to the `Patrol Pts` variable under the script component.

    This will expose the `Size` variable, which sets the size of the array.

12. Set the `Size` value to `2`.

    This will create two new `Element` fields, which will accept any transforms that are dragged onto them.

13. Drag `wayPoint01` from the **Hierarchy** panel onto the `Element 0` field and `wayPoint02` onto the `Element 1` field.

If you press the **Play** button at this point, you should see the zombie move between the two points.

Next, we will make the necessary changes to the animator controller and implement the zombie's animation.

Modifying the animator

The current animator controller is set up the same as we left it at the end of *Chapter 6, Talking Heads*. We need to make a few changes to get the animation running a little more smoothly:

1. In the **Hierarchy** panel, select the `zombie_f` game object.

2. Click on the **Animator** tab in the top center of the main Unity interface to open the **Animator** window.

   The currently selected game object's animator controller should be displayed in the window.

3. Drag the **Animator** tab toward the top of the Unity interface to undock it.

4. Position it so that it can be viewed at the same time as the **Game** view.

5. Press the **Play** button to preview the game.

   The zombie walks to the patrol point and idles briefly before beginning her turn animation:

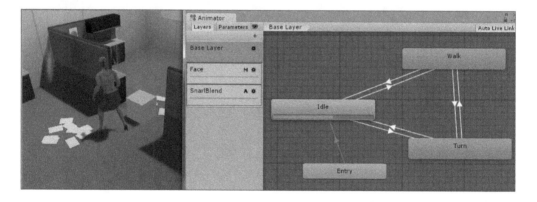

   We can see in the **Animator** window that the zombie is in her **Idle** state even though she is turning toward the next patrol point in the **Game** view.

   This would look better if we reduced the amount of `idle` and got straight to the turn.

6. Press the **Play** button again to exit play mode.

7. In the **Animator** window, click on the **Idle | Turn** transition to view its settings in the **Inspector** panel.

8. Uncheck the **Has Exit Time** checkbox.

   This will interrupt the **Idle** animation and transition straight to **Turn** before the **Idle** cycle has finished playing.

9. Press the **Play** button again to view the result.

At the moment when the zombie walks forward, she does so at a constant rate. In the next step, we will integrate this forward movement better with the animation using an animation curve.

Adding and accessing an animation curve

When the zombie walks forward, the forward movement is defined by a fixed value in the walkSpeed variable.

We can also create a variable tied to the animation frames in the animation's **Import** settings.

Start by locating the walk animation clip in the project:

1. In the **Project** panel, click on the PACKT_Animation folder to view its contents in the **Assets** panel.

2. Locate the zombie_walk asset and click on it once to view its properties in the **Inspector** panel.

3. In the **Inspector** panel, click on the **Animation** tab, if it is not already active.

4. In the list of clips, select zwalk01f.

   The selected animation can be viewed in the **Animation Preview** panel at the bottom.

5. If this panel appears empty, drag the zombie_f game object from the **Hierarchy** panel onto this panel to preview the animation with this character.

6. Scroll to the bottom of the **Inspector** panel and click on the small arrow next to **Curves**.

   By default, there are no curves associated with the animation.

7. Click on the **+** symbol to create a curve.

   You should see an empty timeline proportionately representing the selected motion clip.

8. Rename the new curve ForwardMovement.

9. Click on the curve graph.

   This will open the new curve in the **Curve** window so that it can be edited.

   In the **Curve** window, you can create keyframes by right-clicking on anywhere on the curve and selecting **Add Key** from the pop-up menu.

10. Using the **Animation Preview** panel as a guide, define positive values in the curve, where the zombie should be moving forward.

    The value scale on the left will define the actual forward movement of the zombie per second, so keyframe your maximum value at 1.0.

Remember that the curve represents the **root movement** – the whole body, not the feet.

11. When you are finished defining the curve, set the start and end tangents to **Loop** by clicking on the tangent mode (set by default to **Clamp**) in the **Curve** window and defining **Loop** from the drop-down list.

    This will ensure that the sequence blends together smoothly as the walk cycles.

12. Save the **Import** settings and store the new animation curve by clicking on the **Apply** button at the bottom of the **Inspector** panel:

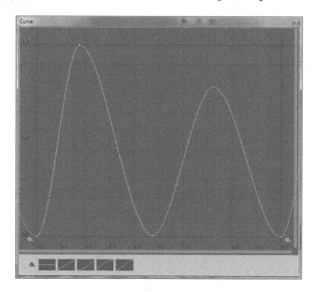

In this curve, I have defined the peaks, where the zombie is propelled forward, and a slight dip at the mid, crossing point of the walk cycle.

Accessing the animation curve in Mecanim and using it in the script

Now that we have added the animation curve to the motion clip, we can make use of it in our Mecanim setup.

We will start by storing the curve's value in the animator controller:

1. In Unity, click on the **Animator** tab to view the zombie's controller.

2. At the top right of the **Animator** panel, click on the **Parameter** tab to activate it.

3. At the moment, we have boolean parameters to trigger the **Walk** and **Turn** states.

4. Create a new parameter by clicking on the **+** symbol.

5. Choose **Float** from the drop-down selection list that appears.

6. Rename the new float parameter ForwardMovement.

   It is important that we give it the same name as the animation curve we created in the **Import** settings, for Mecanim to make a connection between them.

   We can test this, by running the game at this point.

7. Press the **Play** button.

8. Switch to the **Animator** tab, while **Play** mode is still running.

   While the zombie is in her **Walk** state, you should see the value of ForwardMovement change.

The value is grayed out, indicating that it is a read only parameter — it is being driven by the animation curve:

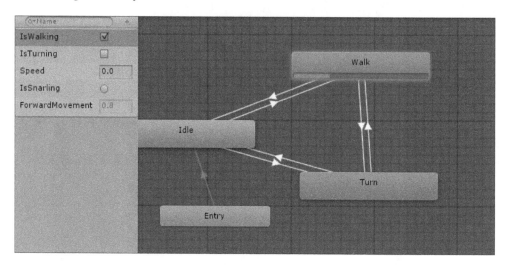

At the moment, this parameter is not affecting the zombie's movement. We need to make another change to the script to effect this.

9. Maximize MonoDevelop and make sure that `zombie_chapter9_Start` is the active script.

10. Add the following code to the top of the `Update` function:

```
var speedFactor = theAnimator.GetFloat("ForwardMovement");

speed = walkSpeed * speedFactor;
```

Here, we create a new local variable to handle the animator parameter, which we are driving with the animation curve. We multiply `walkSpeed` by this value.

We put this in `Update` so that it stays current with the value in the controller.

11. Scroll down to the `WalkTowards` function.

12. Replace the definition of the `direction` variable with the following line of code:

```
var direction =
transform.TransformDirection(Vector3.forward * speed);
```

Here, we replace `walkSpeed` with our new adjusted speed value.

13. Save the script.
14. Press the **Play** button to preview the game.

Our zombie should now lurch forward unevenly. Her forward movement is driven by the animation curve and should appear to be in sync with her walk animation.

Adding the attack

Back in *Chapter 1, The Zombie Attacks!*, we set up the male zombie character to attack the player on a key press. To allow our current zombie to attack, we need to be able to target the player and create a new state to handle the attack animation.

The zombie can already locate the player when he comes within a defined range and move toward him. We need to add some more variables to define when the zombie can attack and for how long:

1. Near the top of the script add the following variables:
    ```
    var attackRange : float = 1.5;
    var attacking : boolean = false;
    var attackDuration : float = 2.0;
    var attackTimer : float;
    ```

    The attackRange float is like the changeDistance variable we are already using for our patrol points. It defines a specific range that will be used to trigger the attack.

    We add a boolean, attacking that will allow us to sync up the state change and other implications. The attackDuration and attackTimer floats will allow us to time out the attack and give the player a chance to respond.

2. Locate the if(alerted) statement near the top of the Update function.

3. Within this, add the following line before the other if statements:
    ```
    if(playerDistance <= attackRange && !attacking)
    {
        Attack();
    }
    ```

    This will run the Attack function. Importantly, we make this dependent on two conditions, the player must be within the range and the boolean attacking is currently false. This will make sure that we do not trigger an attack when we are already attacking.

4. Add the following code next:

```
if(attacking)
{
        attackTimer -= Time.deltaTime;
        if(attackTimer <= 0.0)
        {
            attacking = false;
        }
}
```

Our condition here is that the `attacking` boolean should be `true`. When this is the case, we reduce `attackTimer` by real time. When this reaches zero or below, we set the `attacking` boolean to `false`, timing out the attack.

5. Scroll to the bottom of the script and add the following code:

```
function Attack()
{
    theAnimator.SetTrigger("IsAttacking");
    attackTimer = attackDuration;
    attacking = true;
}
```

Within the actual `Attack` function, we first set a `IsAttacking` trigger to transition into the **Attack** state.

We reset `attackTimer` to the same value as `attackDuration`. If the `Attack` function has already run, this value will be at zero.

We also set the boolean `attacking` to true, which will allow us to run some other code to damage the player.

6. Save the script and return to the main Unity interface.

At this point, we need to add the state to handle the attack animation.

Adding the Attack state

We want the **Attack** state to take priority over the others and to be triggered from any state. Rather than setting up three different transitions, we can just use the **Any State**:

1. Locate **Any State**, in the **Animator** graph.

2. Right-click on an empty part of the graph close to this and choose **Create State | Empty**.

3. Click on the new state and rename it `Attack` in the **Inspector** panel.

4. In the **Project** panel, click on the `PACKT_Animations` folder to view its contents in the **Assets** panel.

5. Locate the `zombie_attack` asset and click on the small arrow next to its icon to expand it.

6. Drag the `hit` animation clip into the motion field of the **Attack** state.

7. Create a transition from the **Any State** box to the new **Attack** state.

   We need to create the new parameter in order to complete this transition.

8. In the top left of the **Animator** panel, click on the **Parameters** tab if it is not already active.

9. Click on the + symbol to create a new parameter and choose **Trigger** from the drop-down list.

10. Rename the new parameter `IsAttacking`.

11. Select the transition between **Any State** and **Attack** and set its condition to `IsAttacking`.

12. Create a transition between **Attack** and **Idle**.

13. Leave its **Condition** empty, it will default to **Exit Time** so that the zombie will begin idling once it has attacked once.

Refer to the following screenshot:

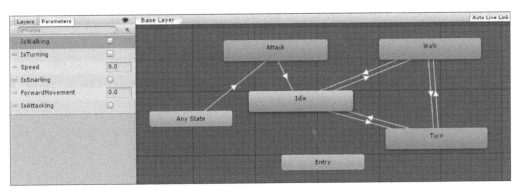

If we test the game at this point, we should see the zombie attack when it is approached. If the player moves away, the zombie will follow the player and try to attack. Before we can allow the zombie to actually harm the player we will assign some tags.

Associating tags with the enemy and player game objects

Now that we have our state machine up and running, it seems like a good time for some consequences.

We can start this using Unity's **tags** to define the `zombie_f` game object as an enemy and `FPSController` as a player.

Tags allow us to define how specific objects or groups of objects are treated. In this case, we want the zombie to send a message to the player to deduct damage when he is hit. If the zombie hits another collider or misses the player, we do not want to send the same message:

1. In the **Hierarchy** panel, click on the `FPSController` game object to select it.

2. In the **Inspector** panel, click on the **Tag** drop-down list in the upper left of the panel.

3. Select **Player** from the list.

4. Back in the **Hierarchy** panel, select the `zombie_f` game object.

5. In the **Inspector** panel, assign the **Enemy** tag to this object.

   We are assigning the player as the zombie's target by dragging the game object into the variable slot in the game scene.

   It seems reasonable to do this for one or two enemies in a single level, but for more than this, it would be handy if the enemy could find the player automatically. We can do this with the tags.

6. Open the `zombie_chapter9_Start` script in MonoDevelop.

7. At the top of the `Start` function, add the following line of code:

   ```
   target = GameObject.FindWithTag ("Player").transform;
   ```

   We use the `GameObject.FindWithTag` method to locate a game object in the scene with the tag **Player**. We then return its transform.

8. Save the script.

9. Back in the main Unity interface, select the `zombie_f` game object in the **Hierarchy** panel.

10. In the **Inspector** panel, click on the radio button next to the **Target** variable slot under the script component.

11. When the **Select Transform** window appears, scroll to the top and select **None**.

    The `target` variable will now be defined at runtime.

12. Press the **Play** button to preview the game at this point and check that this works.

The tags are now setup and the zombie targets the player in the scene automatically.

Allowing the zombie to hurt the player

Now that we have set up the tags, we will continue adding code to the script in MonoDevelop.

1. Add the following variable to the **others** near the top of the `zombie_chapter9_Start` script:

   ```
   var damage: int = 2;
   ```

   This variable will be used to set the amount of damage caused to the player in each attack.

2. Scroll down to the `Attack` function and add the following lines of code:

   ```
   var playerStatus =
   target.Find("FirstPersonCharacter/player_m");
       playerStatus.SendMessage("AddDamage", damage);
   ```

    The `SendMessage` method is a typical way to hurt a player or an enemy and relies on the game object containing a function named `AddDamage` in one of its scripts.

   Back in *Chapter 3, Interacting with the Environment*, we added a simple player status script that allowed our player to receive health power ups. We are accessing this script to damage the player.

   Here, we send the `AddDamage` message with the integer variable `damage` to the game object `player_m`, which the `playerStatus` script is attached to. The `AddDamage` function is run in the script, decreasing the damage.

3. Save the script.

4. In the **Hierarchy** panel, select the `player_m` game object.

5. In the main unity interface, press the **Play** button to preview the game.

6. Walk toward the zombie and allow her to attack the player.

In the **Inspector** panel, we should see the player's health reduced by 2 each time the zombie attacks.

When the player's health is reduced to 0, a message will appear in the console to inform you that the player is dead.

Now that the zombie can attack and hurt the player, we will add the equivalent code to the zombie's script to allow her to be damaged and killed.

Damaging and killing the zombie

In order for our zombie enemy to take damage and ultimately be killed, we need to add a variable that can be decreased when they are struck by the player's bullets:

1. In MonoDevelop, add the following variables to the others, near the top of the zombie_chapter9_Start script:

    ```
    var zombieHealth : int = 5;
    var deadPrefab : Transform;
    ```

    This first new variable stores the current health value. This will decrease when the zombie is hit. We will use deadPrefab to store the ragdoll prefab that we created previously in *Chapter 8, Implementing Ragdoll Physics*.

2. At the bottom of the script, add the following code:

    ```
    function AddDamage(damage : int)
    {
        zombieHealth -= damage;
        if(zombieHealth <= 0)
        {
            zombieHealth = 0;
            Dead();
        }
    }
    ```

    This function is almost identical to the function handling the player's health. When the zombie's health value drops below zero, we call the Dead function, which we will write next.

3. Next, add the following code:

```
function Dead()
{
    Destroy(gameObject);
    if(deadPrefab)
    {
        var dead : Transform = Instantiate(deadPrefab,
        transform.position, transform.rotation);
        CopyTransformsRecurse(transform, dead);
    }
}
static function CopyTransformsRecurse (src : Transform, dst
: Transform)
{
    dst.position = src.position;
    dst.rotation = src.rotation;

    for(var child : Transform in dst)
    {
        var curSrc = src.Find(child.name);
        if(curSrc)
            CopyTransformsRecurse(curSrc, child);
    }
}
```

In the `Dead` function, we destroy the game object — the zombie and all of her components.

We then instantiate the ragdoll, and store this as a local variable named `dead`. We then feed the `dead` prefab and the original transform into a static function named `CopyTransformsRecurse`. This goes through all the child `Transforms` in our original game object and applies their rotation and position to those of the ragdoll, giving us a seamless transition.

To see the result, we need to hook up the ragdoll prefab with the script:

1. Save the script.
2. Select the `zombie_f` game object by clicking on it in the **Hierarchy** panel, if it is not already selected.

3. In the **Inspector** panel, scroll down until you can see the `Zombie chapter9_Start(script)` component.

4. In the **Project** panel, click on the `PACKT_Prefabs` folder to view its contents in the **Assets** panel.

5. Locate the `zombie_f_ragdoll` prefab and drag it into the **Dead Prefab** slot in the `Zombie_chapter9_Start(script)`.

To damage the zombie, we need to fire some bullets, so we will make a small update to the player's script in the next step.

Allowing the player to fire

When the fire button is pressed, a message appears in the console, but the player's weapon does not actually fire any bullets. We will add the necessary code and connect variables to make this happen:

1. In the **Assets** panel, locate `FPSAnimation`.

2. Double-click on it to open it in MonoDevelop.

3. Add the following variables to the top of the script:

```
var bulletPrefab : GameObject;
var muzzle : Transform;
```

Like the ragdoll, the bullet is a prefab that we are instantiating at runtime. This has already been setup.

The next variable, `muzzle`, defines the transform position where the bullet will be instantiated.

4. In MonoDevelop, scroll down until you find the `Shoot` function.

5. Add the following code within its opening and closing brackets:

```
var theBullet = Instantiate(bulletPrefab, muzzle.position,
muzzle.rotation);
theBullet.GetComponent.<Rigidbody>().AddRelativeForce(0, 0,
3000);
```

Here, we assign a new local variable named `theBullet`. We instantiate `bulletPrefab` with the position and rotation of the muzzle transform, within it.

We then add relative force to the object's `rigidbody` component so that it travels in the direction that we fire.

6. Save the script.

7. Minimize MonoDevelop.

8. In the **Project** panel, click on the `PACKT_Prefabs` folder to view its contents in the **Assets** panel.

9. In the **Hierarchy** panel, select the `player_m` game object.

10. Locate `bulletCube` in the **Assets** panel and drag it into the `bulletPrefab` slot under the `FPSAnimation (Script)` component in the **Inspector** panel.

11. In the **Hierarchy** panel, fully expand `player_m` game object's hierarchy by *Alt* + clicking on the small arrow next to its name.

12. Locate the `muzzle` game object (a child of `Gun`) within the `player_m` hierarchy and drag it into the **Muzzle** slot under the `FPSAnimation (Script)` component in the **Inspector** panel.

    The `bulletCube` prefab already has a small script attached to allow it to cause damage with the items it hits.

    To decrease the clutter in our **Scene** view, we can also make the waypoints invisible now that we do not need to see them anymore.

13. Select both waypoint objects in the **Hierarchy** panel.

14. In the **Inspector** panel, uncheck their **Mesh Renderer** components.

They should become invisible in the **Scene** view, though they can still be selected in the hierarchy panel. If we test the game at this point, when we shoot the patrolling zombie, she will drop to the ground lifelessly.

With the values we have set up, it should take three shots to kill a zombie:

In the next section, we will demonstrate how we can use our Mecanim animation setup with navMesh.

Pathfinding and obstacle detection with navMesh

NavMesh is Unity's pathfinding system. It works by defining the navigable areas of the game level, storing this as a simple mesh. Once areas that can be accessed are defined, the navMesh is baked like a lightmap.

This system offers numerous advantages over waypoint systems. Firstly, it allows an AI character to roam freely within a level.

1. Open the scene Chapter9_nav_Start.

    The scene contains the office environment with a navMesh already baked. The steps taken to set this up are well documented on the Unity website.

    We can view the generated navMesh by activating the **Navigation** panel.

2. From the menu bar, choose **Window | Navigation**.

The **Navmesh Display** box will appear in the lower right of the **Scene** view.

By default, the **Show NavMesh** checkbox should be checked and the walkable areas of the game level will be displayed in blue:

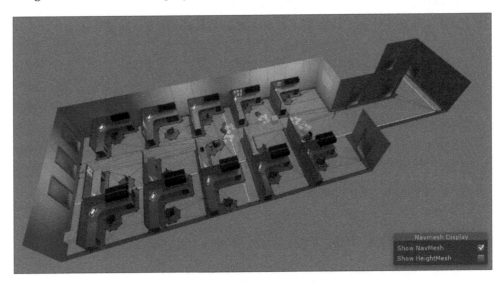

In the scene, the patrol points have been placed to make a more complex route for the zombie. If you press the **Play** button at this point, you will see the zombie walk toward the first point as before.

When she walks toward the second point, she will get stuck as it is not directly in view. We can solve this using Unity's navigation.

Next, we will add the component that will allow the zombie to use the navMesh:

1. In the **Hierarchy** panel, select the `zombie_f_nav` game object.

2. Add a navMesh agent component from the menu bar by navigating to **Component | Navigation | Nav Mesh Agent**.

    The navMesh agent defines how the character moves around the space. It has a `radius` variable, which controls how close the zombie will get to scenery. It also has `speed` and `turning` variables that we will need to set in our script.

    If we test the game at this point, there will be no apparent change, as the navMesh agent requires a goal (or destination) to be set in a script so that a route can be calculated.

3. In the **Project** panel, locate the `PACKT_Scripts` folder and click on it once to view its contents in the **Assets** panel.

4. Open the `zombie_nav_Start` script in MonoDevelop by double-clicking on it in the **Assets** panel.

5. Add the following variables to the others, near the top of the script:

    ```
    var zAgent : NavMeshAgent;
    var navSpeed : float = 1.0;
    ```

    In the `zAgent` variable, we will be storing the navMesh agent so that we can send it other variables. We will use `navSpeed` to keep the speed of the navigation updated.

    In the `Start` function, we will initialize `NavMeshAgent` the same way that we have done with the character controller and animator.

6. Add the following lines of code inside the `Start` function:

    ```
    zAgent = GetComponent (NavMeshAgent);
    ```

    The navMesh agent needs an initial target position to be able to run.

7. Add the following code to the bottom of the function:

    ```
    targetedPt = patrolPts[currPt];
    zAgent.destination = targetedPt.position;
    ```

    Here, we designate the `targetedPt` as the current patrol point. We then define the navMesh agent's destination variable as the `targetedPt` variable's position.

    We also need to make sure that the destination changes when the zombie reaches the patrol point.

8. Add the following line to the top of the `Update` function:

    ```
    zAgent.destination = targetedPt.position;
    ```

    This will be sufficient for the zombie to use the navigation. If you press **Play** at this point, you will see the zombie move rapidly between the two points.

    The navMesh agent has its own internal speed variable. We can keep this the same as the zombie's adjusted walk speed.

9. Add the following code to the `Start` function, directly after the last line that we added:

   ```
   zAgent.speed = navSpeed;
   ```

   We initialize the navMesh agent's `speed` variable, setting it to the value of `navSpeed`. Next, we need to keep this the same as the zombie's adjusted speed value, which changes with the animation.

10. Add the following code to the `Update` function, directly after the last line that we added:

    ```
    navSpeed = speed;
    ```

The zombie will now walk between the patrol points with the corrected speed, but it is not currently being adjusted when she is idling or turning.

The solution is to temporarily suspend the navigation while the zombie is turning.

Suspending navigation during the turn

At this point, we need to slow the zombie down so that she can turn. The best way to do this is to temporarily switch off the navigation.

1. In the `Update` function, locate the `if (ptDistance <= changeDistance)` statement.

   The code contained within this statement will run whenever the zombie comes within the defined range of the patrol point.

2. Add the following code inside the statement's curly brackets:

   ```
   zAgent.Stop();
   ```

   The navMesh agent's `Stop` function will suspend the navigation. We need to resume navigation once the zombie has turned toward the next point.

3. Scroll down to the `WalkTowards` function and add the following code at the start:

   ```
   zAgent.Resume();
   ```

4. Save the script.

If we test the game at this point, we should see the zombie's speed slow long enough for her to execute the turn. If the player comes within range, her attack is relentless and she will pursue the player until she is dead.

In the next step, we will temporarily suspend the navigation while the attack takes place and give the player a chance to escape.

Adjusting navigation during the attack

Currently, when the zombie's attack is initiated, she continues to move toward the player. We can suspend this in the same way that we did for the turn:

1. In the `Update` function, locate the `if(attacking)` statement.

2. Add the following code inside the statement's curly brackets and before the other code:

    ```
    zAgent.Stop();
    ```

The `WalkTowards` function, which runs following the attack, is already setup to resume navigation. If we test the game at this point, the zombie will stop chasing the player when she starts the attack.

The code is currently set up to damage the player whether he is close to the zombie or far away, so we need to add another condition to make sure that the player is close enough to be hurt.

Modifying the Attack function

Here, we will modify the attack to ensure the player is only hurt when he is close enough for the zombie to reach him:

1. Near the top of the script, add the following variable:

    ```
    var playerDamaged : boolean = false;
    ```

    The boolean variable `playerDamaged` will be used as a flag to see if the player is currently being hurt in the attack.

    We only want the player to lose 2 points of health per attack, not to be hurt continuously during the time the attack takes place.

2. In the `Update` function, locate the following `if` statement:

    ```
    if(attackTimer <= 0.0)
    ```

3. Add the following code inside the curly brackets of the statement:

```
playerDamaged = false;
```

4. Directly after the `if` statement, add the following code:

```
if(attackTimer > 0.7 && playerDistance <= attackRange &&
!playerDamaged)
{
    DamagePlayer();
}
```

Here we check that the attack has been going for `0.7` seconds, the `playerDistance` object is within `attackRange`, and the player is not already being damaged.

These are the conditions that need to be met before we damage the player. We move the actual damaging into its own function, `DamagePlayer`.

5. Scroll down to the `Attack` function and locate the last two lines of code:

```
var playerStatus =
target.Find("FirstPersonCharacter/player_m");
playerStatus.SendMessage("AddDamage", damage);
```

6. Select the lines and delete them from the function.

7. After the closing curly bracket of the function, add the following code:

```
function DamagePlayer()
{
    playerDamaged = true;
    var playerStatus =
    target.Find("FirstPersonCharacter/player_m");
    playerStatus.SendMessage("AddDamage", damage);
}
```

Here, we set the boolean `playerDamaged` to `true`.

Next, we add the lines that we deleted from the `Attack` function, connecting to the player status script and applying the damage.

8. Save the script.

If we test the game at this point, we should be able to slip away from the zombie without being damaged after she starts the attack:

Zombies are forgetful creatures; it would be good to allow a zombie to forget about the player after he has been out of range for long enough. We can add this feature to the AI script next.

Timing out the zombie's pursuit

By adding the time out, we allow the zombie to forget about the player after enough time has been spent out of range:

1. Add the following code to the list of variables at the top of the `zombie_nav_Start` script:

   ```
   var alertTimeOut : float = 5.0;
   var alertTimer : float;
   ```

   The variable `alertTimeOut` defines the time in seconds that it will take the zombie to forget about the player. Keeping this variable exposed, makes it easy to adjust in the **Inspector** panel.

   The next variable, `alertTimer`, keeps track of the time that has passed.

2. In the `Update` function, locate the following `if` statement:

    ```
    if(playerDistance <= attackRange && !attacking)
    {
     Attack();
    }
    ```

3. Add the following line of code after `Attack()`:

    ```
    alertTimer = 0.0;
    ```

4. After the closing curly bracket of the statement, add the following code:

    ```
    else if(playerDistance > alertDistance)
    {
        alertTimer += Time.deltaTime;
        if(alertTimer > alertTimeOut)
        {
            alerted = false;
        }
    }
    ```

    The `else if` statement comes into play when `alerted` is `true` and the distance between the zombie and the player is greater than the `alertDistance` value.

    When this is the case, we increase the `alertTimer` by time in seconds, and when this value reaches the `alertTimeOut` value, we set `alerted` to `false`, returning our zombie to her waypoint behavior.

    For cleanliness, we zero out the `alertTimer` in the original `if` statement, so that the increase does not accumulate.

5. Save the script.
6. Test the game by pressing the **Play** button.

The zombie will move between the waypoints and then chase the player when he comes within range. If we are able to get away far enough, the zombie will lose interest in the player and return to her patrol:

There are lots more things we can do here with navMesh and Mecanim. For instance, we can set up a complex level in which multiple zombies have overlapping patrols. The player needs to negotiate to get through the game level.

In Unity, the navMesh toolset has many capabilities for triggering behavior and giving the appearance of intelligence. The pathfinding happens behind the scenes, allowing us to create more realistic and challenging enemy behaviors.

Summary

In this chapter, we developed animation-triggering techniques introduced previously with the objective of creating an enemy that is both responsive and realistic.

We started by implementing range detection in an existing script to give the appearance of the enemy's response to the player.

We set up a simple waypoint system to allow the enemy to patrol the level.

By driving root motion with an animation curve, we connected to Mecanim on a deeper level and were able to better synchronize movement and animation.

Next, we elaborated on the enemy's attack and added the necessary code for it to be injured and killed, implementing the ragdoll effects that we created in *Chapter 8, Implementing Ragdoll Physics*.

Finally, we dealt with obstacle avoidance with Unity's potent navMesh system and coordinated the zombie's attack duration and time out.

In this book, we covered a few different techniques which Mecanim can be harnessed to create powerful and engaging character animation in Unity 5. I hope to have demonstrated that Mecanim is a powerful and dynamic toolset for character animation.

Its visual representation of state machines, and its ability to create complex animation routines, even with very little code make it an essential tool for anyone interested in animation in games.

The potential uses of this toolset are expanding every day with a very large and active user base sharing problems and solutions on Unity's community forums.

Index

Symbol

3ds Max
  rigging process 26

A

animation
  previewing, by adjusting scene elements 21
  previewing, in game view 21
animation curve
  accessing 237-241
  adding 237, 238
  using, in script 239-241
animator controller
  Null state, creating 158, 159
  second layer, creating 142, 143
  setting up 13
  Snarl state, adding 157, 158
  transitions, setting between Null
      and Snarl states 159
  updating, for including face
      animation 156, 157
  updating, to handle blendshape
      animation 177, 179
  used, for driving blendshape
      animation 172
animator controller, setting up
  parameter, creating 16
  script, writing 19, 20
  states, creating 15, 16
  steps 14, 15
  transitions, adding 17019
arm joints, rigging process
  creating 61, 62
  finger joints, cloning 63

Avatar
  bone hierarchy, checking 12, 13
  character's pose, adjusting 11, 12
  creating 7-11
Avatar Body Masks
  new scene, opening 138-142
  working with 138
Avatar masks
  adding 147, 148

B

biped's parameters
  adjusting 29, 30
  adjusting, to fit character 30
  bone display colors, changing 32
  bones, orienting to match
      character model 33
  bones, renaming 36
  bones, scaling to match character model 33
  character mesh, freezing 31, 32
  joints, repositioning for jaw 34
  joints, repositioning for pony tail 34
  limb positions, adjusting 35
  shortcuts, using 36-38
  X-ray mode, switching to 31, 32
blended animation
  collectable prefabs, instancing 196, 197
  previewing 198
  testing, in game 196
blendshape animation
  driving, with animator controller 172
  face blendshape, keyframing 175, 176
  handling, by updating
      animator controller 177
  viewing, in Unity 173-175

Blend Tree

about 181

accommodating, by updating character
script 187

adding, to player's existing animator
controller 182

blended animation, testing 196

blending graph 184

character animation script, editing 193, 194

Collectable script, updating 194, 195

creating, in Pickup state 191

motion clips, adding 184, 185

motions group 184

objectWeight variable, sending 195

parameter 184

parameters, adding 185-187

parameters, adjusting 186, 187

pickup Blend Tree parameter,
setting up 192

properties, using 183, 184

testing, in game view 188, 189

thresholds, adding 186, 187

thresholds, adjusting 186, 187

threshold, setting for pickup
Blend Tree 192, 193

used, for adding strafing animation to
player character 182, 183

used, for varying pickup animation 189

C

character

skinning, with skin modifier 38-40

character animation script

Pick function, updating 195

updating, for using Blend Tree 187

character joints

fine tuning 217

rotational limits of forearm, adjusting 219

rotational limits of head, adjusting 220

rotational limits of upper arm,
adjusting 218

character, skinning

default pose, saving 40, 41

selection set, creating 40

skin modifier, using 38-40

test pose, creating 41-44

collectable objects

adding 92

implementing 92

lunchbox collectable, instantiating into
game level 92

lunchbox collectable's components,
inspecting 93

lunchbox collectable, testing 108, 109

player character's response, setting up 95

Collectable script

updating, for including
weight variable 194, 195

collision objects

adjusting 213

capsule collider radius, adjusting 213, 214

head's collider, adjusting 214-216

considerations, modeling

mesh density 25

polycount 25

Quads and Triangles 25

cross sections 46

custom joint, adding to ragdoll object

about 221

capsule collider,
adding to ponytail 221, 222

character joint, adding 223

Rigidbody component, adding 222

E

Edge Loop 25

enemy

Avatar, creating 7

importing 2, 3

import scale, adjusting 4-7

material, organizing 3

rig import settings, adjusting 7

textures, organizing 3

F

FBX files 3

female zombie character

snarl face animation, adding 152

First-Person Shooter (FPS) 78

five walk variations
  creating, from walk cycles 146, 147
Forward Kinematics (FK) 42

G

GameObject.FindWithTag method 244
Generic format 8
GetComponent method 124

H

hinge joint
  adding 204-206
Humanoid animation 9
Humanoid Avatar 24
Humanoid format 7, 8

I

import settings
  adjusting 130
  duplicate walk cycle, creating 131
  motion parameters, adjusting 131-134
  muscle limits, adjusting 134-137
initial ragdoll
  bones, assigning to list 209, 210
  default ragdoll, previewing 212
  generating 209
  mass, assigning 210
Inverse Kinematics (IK) 26, 42
IsSnarling parameter
  creating 160
isTurning parameter
  setting 164
  transitions, creating to connect
    turning state 165

J

joints, Unity
  about 202
  hinge joint, adding 204-206
  test scene, creating 202-204

L

legacy format 7
leg and arm chains, rigging process
  connecting 65
  jaw joints, creating 65
  joint transforms, aligning 66, 67
  mirroring 64
  ponytail, creating 65
  test pose, creating 67, 68
lunchbox collectable's components
  collectable script, viewing 93
  inspecting 93
  self destruction, implementing 94, 95

M

material, ragdoll object
  assigning 208
  character joints, fine tuning 217
  collision objects, adjusting 212
  custom joint, adding 221
  initial ragdoll, generating 209
  ragdoll, saving as prefab 224
  rotational head limits, adjusting 220
Maya
  rigging process 54
Mecanim
  about 8, 75
  Humanoid animation type 151
modeling
  considerations 25
  for animation 25
motion capture
  characteristics 112
  sequences, creating 112
motion capture sequence
  adjusting, in Animations tab 118, 119
  creating 112
  importing 114
  import settings, adjusting 114
  rig import settings, adjusting 116-118
  second walk cycle, creating 121
  using, with pre-rigged model 113

N

navMesh
  Attack function, modifying 254-256
  navigation, adjusting 254
  navigation, suspending during turn 253
  used, for obstacle detection 250-253
  used, for pathfinding 250-252
ngons 25

O

objectWeight variable
  sending 195

P

patrol behavior
  initial patrol code, adding 231-234
  setting up 229
  variables, adding 230
Pick function
  about 104
  updating, in character animation script 195
pickup animation
  pickup_heavy animation sequence,
      viewing 190, 191
  varying, with Blend Tree 189
pickup Blend Tree parameter
  setting 192
Pickup state
  adding, to animator controller 96
  Blend Tree, creating 191
  parameter, adding 97
  parameter, creating 97
  shoot Idle and Pickup states,
      transitioning 96
  transitions and parameter, setting 96
player's character response
  Collectable script, updating 101, 102
  FPSAnimation script, updating 104
  pickup camera, creating 98
  pickup camera prefab, finalizing 98, 99
  pickup script, modifying 104-107
  Pickup state, adding to
      animator controller 96
  player status script, adding
      to game object 101

  player status script, viewing 100, 101
  setting up 95-103
  variables, hooking up in
      collectable script 103, 104
pre-rigged model
  motion capture sequence, using with 113
project assets package
  animator controller, modifying 87
  camera height, adjusting 80, 81
  camera setup, completing 86
  character animation script,
      implementing 89
  character animation script, writing 89
  character controller, adding 78-80
  first person rig, saving as prefab 84
  gun, adding 82, 83
  gun, parenting 82, 83
  importing 76
  initial code, adding to FPSAnimation
      script 89, 90
  new scene, creating 77
  office-level scene, adding 84-86
  player character model,
      adding to scene 77, 78
  player character, setting up 76
  script, adding to player character
      game object 91
  shoot idle animation, adding 81, 82
  transition, setting 87
  trigger parameter, creating
      for Shoot state 88, 89

R

ragdoll object
  adjusted ragdoll, previewing 220
  creating 206, 207
  material, assigning 208
ragdoll physics 201
Ragdoll Wizard 209
range detection
  animation curve, accessing 237, 238
  animation curve, adding 237, 238
  animator, modifying 236
  attack, adding 241, 242
  fire button, using by player 248-250
  implementing 225

initial AI script, adding 227
patrol behavior, setting up 229
patrol code, defining 234, 235
proximity detection, adding to enemy AI
     script 227-229
scene, opening 226
zombie attack, adding 241
zombie, damaging 246, 247
zombie, killing 246, 247
Reference Coordinate System 33
rigging process, 3ds Max
about 26
biped's parameters, adjusting 29, 30
biped system, creating 28, 29
character, exporting 53, 54
character model, importing 27, 28
character, skinning with
     skin modifier 38-40
need for 23
requisites 24
scene, setting up 26, 27
rigging process, Maya
about 54
arm joints, creating 61
character mesh, binding to skeleton 69, 70
display grid size, modifying 55
exporting, for Unity 73, 74
joints, creating for back 58, 59
joints, creating for head 58, 59
joints, creating for neck 58, 59
joints, mirroring for arm chains 64
joints, mirroring for leg 64
joints, renaming 59, 60
joints, repositioning 59, 60
leg joints, creating 60, 61
model, importing 55, 56
model scale, adjusting 56, 57
setting up 54
skin weights, painting 71, 72
system units, setting to meters 55
toolset, adjusting for joint creation 57, 58
viewport display, adjusting for joint
     creation 57, 58
rig import settings
adjusting 7
appropriate rig import settings,
     selecting 7-9

Generic 7
Humanoid 7
Legacy 7
root movement 238

S

scene
animation, adding 128-130
animation, previewing 128-130
Avatar Body Masks, working 138
import settings, adjusting 130
loading 128
second layer, creating in
     animation controller 142
scene elements
adjusting, for animation preview 21
second layer, animator controller
creating 142, 143
masked animation, previewing 145, 146
parameter, setting in mask layer 144
script, editing 144, 145
states, creating in mask layer 143
transitions, setting in mask layer 144
second walk cycle
animation switch, previewing 124, 125
creating 121
new motion clips, adding to animation
     controller 122, 123
script, adding 124, 125
walk animation loops difference, checking
     with script 123, 124
selection set, 3ds Max
creating 40
SendMessage method 245
shoot idle sequence 81
skin modifier
adjustments, making 44
Envelopes, adjusting 45-47
influence, adjusting on head vertices 47-51
skin weights, painting for jaw bone 51, 52
used, for skinning character 38-40
skinning process 38
snarl face animation
adding, to female zombie character 152
scene, adding 152

Snarl function
  creating 169
sourcing models 25
Start function 124

T

transform.LookAt method 162
Transitions 15
transitions, setting between
        Null and Snarl states
  about 159
  IsSnarling parameter, creating 160
  script, editing for including
        Face layer 160, 161
  zombie's turn rotation, smoothing 162, 163
turn animation
  implementing 163
  isTurning parameter, setting 164
  state, adding 163, 164
  transitions, setting for turn state 165
TurnToPlayer function
  adding 154

U

Unity
  joints 202
Unity Asset Store
  about 25
  URL 25
Unity Input Manager 90
Unity project
  animation, previewing by adjusting scene
        elements 21
  animator controller, setting up 13

enemy, importing 2
setting up 1, 2
Update function 20, 144

V

Vector3.Distance method 228

W

WaitForSeconds method 103
Wavefront OBJ format 27

Y

yield WaitForSeconds method 154

Z

zombie attack
  adding 241, 242
  Attack state, adding 242, 243
  code, adding to MonoDevelop script 245
  tags, associating with enemy 244
  tags, associating with player
        game objects 244
  time out, adding 256-258
zombie_ready script
  code, adding 152, 153
  Snarl function, creating 169
  snarl sound, synchronizing 170-172
  TurnToPlayer function, adding 154
  updating, for accommodating
        turn state 166-169
  variables, connecting,
        in Inspector panel 155, 156

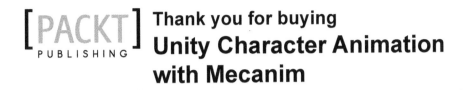

Thank you for buying
Unity Character Animation with Mecanim

About Packt Publishing

Packt, pronounced 'packed', published its first book, *Mastering phpMyAdmin for Effective MySQL Management*, in April 2004, and subsequently continued to specialize in publishing highly focused books on specific technologies and solutions.

Our books and publications share the experiences of your fellow IT professionals in adapting and customizing today's systems, applications, and frameworks. Our solution-based books give you the knowledge and power to customize the software and technologies you're using to get the job done. Packt books are more specific and less general than the IT books you have seen in the past. Our unique business model allows us to bring you more focused information, giving you more of what you need to know, and less of what you don't.

Packt is a modern yet unique publishing company that focuses on producing quality, cutting-edge books for communities of developers, administrators, and newbies alike. For more information, please visit our website at www.packtpub.com.

Writing for Packt

We welcome all inquiries from people who are interested in authoring. Book proposals should be sent to author@packtpub.com. If your book idea is still at an early stage and you would like to discuss it first before writing a formal book proposal, then please contact us; one of our commissioning editors will get in touch with you.

We're not just looking for published authors; if you have strong technical skills but no writing experience, our experienced editors can help you develop a writing career, or simply get some additional reward for your expertise.

Unity 5 for Android Essentials

Unity 5 for Android Essentials

ISBN: 978-1-78439-919-1   Paperback: 200 pages

A fast-paced guide to building impressive games and applications for Android devices with Unity 5

1. Design beautiful effects, animations, physical behaviors, and other different real-world features for your Android games and applications.

2. Optimize your project and any other real-world projects for Android devices.

3. Follows a tutorial-based approach to learning the best practices for accessing Android functionality, rendering high-end graphics, and expanding your project using Asset Bundles.

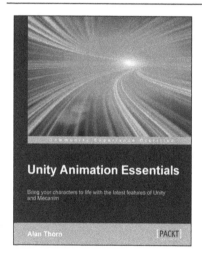

Unity Animation Essentials

Unity Animation Essentials

ISBN: 978-1-78217-481-3   Paperback: 200 pages

Bring your characters to life with the latest features of Unity and Mecanim

1. Learn the latest features of Unity 5 to develop the most amazing animations for all types of games.

2. Refine your character animations by applying more advanced workflows and techniques with Mecanim.

3. A comprehensive book that explores core animation concepts and demonstrates their practical application in games.

Please check **www.PacktPub.com** for information on our titles

Building Levels in Unity

ISBN: 978-1-78528-284-3   Paperback: 274 pages

Create exciting 3D game worlds with Unity

1. Craft game environments with extreme clarity by adding realism to characters, objects, and props.

2. Import and set up custom assets such as meshes, textures, and normal maps in Unity.

3. A step-by-step guide written in a practical format to take advantage of the many features available in Unity.

Getting Started with Unity 5

ISBN: 978-1-78439-831-6   Paperback: 184 pages

Leverage the power of Unity 5 to create amazing 3D games

1. Learn to create interactive games with the Unity 5 game engine.

2. Explore advanced features of Unity 5 to help make your games more appealing and successful.

3. A step-by-step guide giving you the perfect start to developing games with Unity 5.

Please check **www.PacktPub.com** for information on our titles

CPSIA information can be obtained
at www.ICGtesting.com
Printed in the USA
FSHW011241040819
60694FS